NORTH CAROLINA GENERAL ASSEMBLY SESSIONS RECORDS

Slaves and Free Persons of Color 1709–1789

William L. Byrd, III

HERITAGE BOOKS
2011

HERITAGE BOOKS
AN IMPRINT OF HERITAGE BOOKS, INC.

Books, CDs, and more—Worldwide

For our listing of thousands of titles see our website
at
www.HeritageBooks.com

Published 2011 by
HERITAGE BOOKS, INC.
Publishing Division
100 Railroad Ave. #104
Westminster, Maryland 21157

Copyright © 2001 William L. Byrd, III

All rights reserved. No part of this book may be reproduced or transmitted in any form or by any means, electronic or mechanical, including photocopying, recording or by any information storage and retrieval system without written permission from the author, except for the inclusion of brief quotations in a review.

International Standard Book Numbers
Paperbound: 978-0-7884-1963-8
Clothbound: 978-0-7884-8839-9

My beloved brethren: -- The Indians of North and of South America -- the Greeks -- the Irish, subjected under the king of Great Britain -- the Jews, that ancient people of the Lord -- the inhabitants of the islands of the sea -- in fine, all the inhabitants of the earth, (except however, the sons of Africa) are called *men*, and of course are, and ought to be free. But we, (coloured people) and our children are *brutes*!! And of course are, and *ought to be* Slaves to the American people and their children forever!! to dig their mines and work their farms; and thus go on enriching them, from one generation to another with our *blood* and our *tears*!!!! David Walker[1]

---

[1] David Walker, *David Walker's Appeal, In Four Articles; to the Coloured Citizens of the World* (1830; reprint, New York: Hill and Wang, Inc., 1995), 7.

Contents

Introduction _____ *vii*

Acknowledgements _____ *ix*

Chapter One _____ *1*
  General Assembly Sessions _____ 1
    1709 - 1782 _____ 1

Chapter Two _____ *49*
  General Assembly Sessions _____ 49
    1783 - 1789 _____ 49

Chapter Three _____ *93*
  Secretary of State Papers _____ 93
    Magistrates Courts _____ 93

Chapter Four _____ *153*
  Court Martial _____ 153
    Lieut. William Lytle _____ 153

Appendix A _____ *163*
  Table of Cases _____ 163

Appendix B _____ *181*
  North Carolina Laws _____ 181

Index _____ *201*

Introduction

North Carolina's General Assembly Sessions records are teeming with intrigue of every description. They abound with murder, poison, rape, conspiracy, angry pilots, clandestine dealings with slaves, pious Quakers, slaves from Africa, greed, and last, but not least, the ordinary people themselves.

The records are comprised of a vast collection of manuscripts bulging with a wealth of historical documents. They consist of 624.4 cu. ft. of records stored in 1,561 fibredex boxes. The records are arranged chronologically, and by record type.[2]

Some of the documents in this collection are torn, faded, or unreadable. Occasionally, in document groups, a few pages are missing. By and large, they have remained intact since the Colonial era, and loss of records appears to be minimal.

North Carolina's legislature most likely met for the first time in 1665, as the General Assembly of Albemarle County.[3] The transcriptions published in this volume span the years from 1709 to 1789, and represent a wide variety of documents. Every attempt has been made to remain true to the original text.

It would not be proper to assign these papers as solely about African Americans. That would be an understatement. By far, more Whites are represented than Blacks. It is the interaction between Blacks and Whites that is brought forth in this book. Sometimes on good terms, and sometimes on bad terms, they confronted each other like an intricately woven tapestry.

In 1715, the Colony of North Carolina enacted a law that established courts to try slaves who were found guilty of various crimes.

---

[2] *Guide to Research Materials in the North Carolina State Archives: State Agency Records* (Raleigh: Division of Archives and History, Department of Cultural Resources, 1992), 738.

[3] Ibid, 734.

Normally called Magistrates Courts, they consisted of three Justices and three Freeholders, usually owners of slaves.[4] North Carolina probably patterned this law from a similar law passed by the South Carolina Legislature in 1690.[5] These "Special Courts" deprived slaves of the rights available to white colonists. The Judgments were final, and justice was swift. The effect was total control over the slave population. Masters of slaves were compensated from the Public Treasury for slaves that were executed, or who were shot and killed while being apprehended.[6]

Chief Justice Martin Howard denounced this new policy of eliminating due process. He stated that; "three Justices and four Freeholders ... may despatch a negro slave into the other world, with very little ceremony, for a fault which the naked, half-starved wretch had, perhaps, been forced to commit, because of the rigor or covetousness of his master."[7]

During the next fifty years, after the Revolution, slaves in North Carolina achieved the right of trial by jury in some cases. They were also given the right to appeal conviction.[8]

A Table of Cases for the Magistrates Courts records is provided in Appendix A. Appendix B contains the laws relative to the Magistrates Courts between the years of 1715 and 1825.

Other records included besides Magistrates Courts records are: petitions to import slaves, Quaker petitions, hiring slaves for the public, free negro petitions, petitions regarding pilots, slaves carried off by the British enemy, a Mecklenburg County petition regarding slaves for compensation instead of money to American troops, slaves from Africa and the Carribean, emancipation papers, and a variety of other documents.

---

[4] Donna J. Spindel, *Crime and Society in North Carolina, 1663-1776* (Baton Rouge: Louisiana State University Press, 1989), 20.
[5] Alan D. Watson, "North Carolina Slave Courts, 1715-1785," *North Carolina Historical Review* 60 (January 1983): 35.
[6] Donna J. Spindel, *Crime and Society in North Carolina, 1663-1776* (Baton Rouge: Louisiana State University Press, 1989) 20.
[7] Marvin L. Kay and Lorin Lee Cary, *Slavery in North Carolina, 1748-1775* (Chapel Hill: The University Press of North Carolina, 1995), 71.
[8] Alan D. Watson, "North Carolina Slave Courts, 1715-1785," *North Carolina Historical Review* 60 (January 1983): 35-36.

Acknowledgements

Acknowledgements for this book are due to the ever helpful staff of the North Carolina State Archives. Their courteous help and attention made this publication possible.

General Assembly Sessions Records
1709-1782

Chapter One

General Assembly Sessions

1709 - 1782

North Carolina State Archives
General Assembly Sessions Records
1709-1760, Box #1

Will, a slave

1739
[Partial Record] [Magistrates Court Record]
Edgecombe County planter with ffeloniously brakeing open his house and takeing from thence Sundry Goods The said John Burny being Sworn on the Holy Evangelist Deposes that the Jacket Britches & hatt & Stockings & Shoes the said Negro Will now has upon him were Stole from him the deponent when his house was brocken open. The Negro Says he got the Said Cloths from John Huces

The above Justice & ffreeholders haveing considred the above evidence do unanimously find the said Negro Will Guilty of the ffellony accused with and ordain that he be carried to the next convenient Tree and there hanged up by the neck till he be dead. The said Justices & ffreeholders

General Assembly Sessions Records 1709-1782

then considered the value of the said Negro and do unanimusly agree and Value the said Negro at Two hundred pounds money of this province.
David Coltrane   JP
JG Cordy[?]   JP
[?]Land Williams
Js Lane
Richard Lewis
Wm Williams

Committee of Claims

Essex, a Slave

March-April, 1740-41
Apl. 3rd 1740
Mr. Thomas Barker moved to be allowed for a Negro Man named Essex who was Condemned and executed in Bertie for a felony by him Comitted - The Sd Claim was allowed - 200.

Committee of Claims

Davie, a Slave

Apl. 3rd 1740
Carolina for a negro Man which belonged to sd Isaac Nichols Named Davie which Negro Man was executed at Pasquotank for a felony by him Committed   allowed the sum of - 175.

Committee of Claims

Nedd, a Slave

Wm Hoskins was allow'd for a Negro man Slave named Nedd who was arraigned & convicted and Executed for Burglary & felony at Edenton 28th day of Decmr. 1741 wch said Negro was valued at £33.6.8 proc.

General Assembly Sessions Records
1709-1782

money.Richard McClure was allowed for taking the minutes on the tryal of a Negro man of Wm. Hoskins & writing the death Warrant .5.-

---

Committee of Claims

George, a Slave

3 Oct 1751
John Macon of Granville County was Allowed for a Negro Man Slave Called georg belonging to him Executed for Felony in the said County. the sum of £42.10
And Whereas Coll. William Eaton produced an Order from the said John Macon to receive the Said Sum it is the Opinion of Your Committee that the said sum be paid to him.

Committee of Claims

Tom, a Slave

30 Sep 1755
Allowed to Capt. John DuBois for a Negro Man named Tom who was Executed for a Felony in New Hanover County - 70.0.0

Committee of Claims

Tony, a Slave

Oct 14, 1756
George Moore Esqr. allowed his Claim of Seventy Pounds Proclamation Money for a Negro Man Named Tony who was Killed in the apprehending; Valued in the County Court of New Hanover as by their Certificate thereof.

Magistrates Court Records

General Assembly Sessions Records 1709-1782

Charles, a Slave

1759

For the Tryall of a Certain Negro Man Named Charles a Slave Belonging to William Pratt Pursuant to the Several Acts of General Assembly of the aforesaid Province.

[The rest of this document is badly torn]

North Carolina }
Craven County }

in New Bern on [**Torn**   ]
Second Year of the Reign of our Sovereign [**Torn**   ]
the Grace of God of Great Brittain France Ireland [**Torn**   ]
Defender of the Faith and so forth. And in the Year of our Lord one Thousand Seven Hundred and Fifty Eight

For the Tryal of a Certain Negro Man Named Charles a Slave Belonging to William Pratt Pursuant to the Several Acts of General Assembly of the aforesaid Province

                       Present

The Worships   Jos Leech[?]   } Esqrs. Justices & owners
             Jas. Davis   } of Slaves Duly Sworn
               &   }
           Andrew [?]tt   }

Mr Ja**[Torn]**   Green Senr.   }
Mr. Thomas Graves   } Gentlemen Freeholders and
Mr James Parkinson   } Owners of slaves duly
Sworn
Mr. John Rice   }

Joseph Carruthers Esqr. Sheriff and Peter Conway   Ck Cur.
The Sheriff Ordered to set the Prisoner at the Barr   Done
[Torn]   ] Arraigned and Pleaded
[Torn]   ] three Weeks ago her

General Assembly Sessions Records
1709-1782

[Torn   ] and that there was Stole [Torn   ] house at the [?] time Eight Yards of Striped [Torn   ] She Bought from Mr. Richard Graham and paid him for the same Two Pounds five Shillings which said Linning now Produced at the Barr and found, in the Prisoners Custody She Swears to be the same Linning Stole from her

2d. Evidence Charged was Dick a Negro belonging to James Williams Saith that he was Siting down at [Torn] Window in a New House Belonging to Doctor Scott[?] in New Bern and that he seen the Prisoner at the Barr and Jno. Fontaines Negro Wench at a Well and that the Prisoner Came in to him and staid

there some time and left a Bag with [Torn] things in it with him, among which things in said Bag [Torn] the Stamp   Linning Produced at the Barr Belonging to the aforesaid Margaret McCoy

3d. Evidence Sworn Elizabeth Fontaine Saith That about the same time that Margaret McCloys Linning was stole from her, that her the said Elizabeth Fontaines Kitchen was Broken Open at Night & that a Box Belonging to a Negro Wench of hers was Broke Open and out of it Taken a shirt and Pockett Book and Sundry other things which were returned in Six or Seven Days after by Wm. Pratt the Prisoners Master who found them in the Prisoners Possession   Sundry other Evidence Sworn and Charged Saith Much to the same Purpose as the forgoing Evidences.

Whereupon as well the Justices as the Freeholders having Maturely and Deliberately Weighed and Considered Matter Procedded to Give Judgment Which was as follows to Wit   That the Sheriff Take the said Negro Man Charles Prisoner at the Barr, Back to the Place from whence he Came / being the Precinct Thereto [?   ] Untill Saturday the Twenty sixth Day of August One Thousand Seven hundred and Fifty Eight Then to be Down to the Common Place of Execution for Malefactors and there to be hanged by the Neck Untill his Body is Dead.

And their Worships and Freeholders Ascertain the Value of the said Negro be Seventy five Pounds Proclamation money In Witness Whereof their Worships and Freeholders have Hereunto Set their hands and Seals
Jams. Green Senr. F.   (Seal   Jos Leech J.P.   (Seal)

General Assembly Sessions Records
1709-1782

Thos. Graves   F.   (Seal)   Jas. Davis J.P.   (Seal)
Jams. Parkinson   (Seal)   Andr. Scott J.P.   (Seal)
Jno. Rice   (Seal)

The foregoing is a True Copy of the Tryall of the afd. Negr. Man Charles Belonging to Wm. Pratt
        Test Peter Conway Clk Cur.
This may Certify that the Said negro Charles was Executed according to the within Sentance
                Jos Carruthers Sher.

****

North Carolina State Archives
General Assembly Sessions Records
April-May, 1760, Box #2
Committee of Claims

Tom, a Slave

16 April 1761
Mr. Joseph Watters was Alowed the Sum of Sixty Pounds Prockl. Money for a Negroe man Call'd Tom Condemned Agreeable to an Act of Assembly of this Province directing the Tryals of Slaves the said Negroe Sence Reprieved by his Excellency. The Committee are of oppinion that the House order him to be Stripd of by the treasurer to Reimburse the Public.

Committee of Claims

Jack, a Slave

16 April 1761
Mr: John Dalrymple was Allowed the sum of Sixty Pounds Prock. Money for a Negroe man Calld Jack which was shot Braking his Masters House And Being Run away.

General Assembly Sessions Records
1709-1782

Committee of Claims

Cyrus & Sampson, Slaves

16 April 1761
Weight & Mortimore was Allowed their Claim of Eight Pounds For Castrating and Attending of Two Slaves Vizt Cyrus belonging to Darby Eugan, Sampson Belonging to Job How the Sheriff having given up his right.

Committee of Claims

Quaugh, a Slave

16 April 1761
Mr. John Mortimore was Allowed his Claim of Four pounds Prock. Money for Castrating and Attending of a Negroe Called Quaugh the Property of Mr. Dry the Sheriff having given up his right.

Committee of Claims

Negroe fellow, a Slave

16 April 1761
Mr. John Walker was Allowed his Claim of one Pound Nineteen Shillings and Four pence For burning A Negroe Fellow in Duplin and Sundrie Other Services &C.

Committee of Claims
16 April 1761
Mr. William Walker was Allowed his Claim of Four Pounds sixteen shillings and Eight pence For Executing Two Negroes and Sundrie other services &c.

Committee of Claims

General Assembly Sessions Records 1709-1782

16 April 1761
Your Committee recommends to the House that a proper Allowance be made for the taking of an Indian Scalp Produced by Mr. John Frohock, taken by Henry Harmon who went with a partie under the Command of Captn. Trag[?] -- Allowed by the House - 10.0.0.

Committee of Claims
16 April 1761
Cornelius Harnett Esqr. Was Allowed his claim of One Pound nine shillings & Eight Pence for holding an Inquest on the Body of one Mena Portagees he having paid the Jurors and other Charges &c.

Committee of Claims

Tom, a Slave

29 April 1762
John Oliver was allowed thirty pounds being the Valuation Money for a Negroe Man, called Tom, to him belonging, Who was tried by the Special Court in Craven County, And Judgment that he should be castrated, which being put in Execution died by means of the Operation in a Short time after.

Committee of Claims

Jack, a Slave

29 April 1762
John Roberts was allowed his Claim of Sixty pounds being the Valuation Money, for a Negroe called Jack, who was executed for Felony at Newbern being the Second Offence.

Committee of Claims

General Assembly Sessions Records
1709-1782

Jack, a Slave

29 April 1762
William Halsey Sheriff of Chowan County was allowed four pounds for castrating a Negroe called Jack, belonging to Joshua Bodiley Esqr. Which is the allowance by Law, as p acct. filed.

Committee of Claims

Cato, a Slave

29 April 1762
Richard Spaight Esqr. Was allowed his claim of Sixty pounds being the valuation Money, for a Negroe Man Slave to him belonging, called Cato, who had been outlawed and wounded in apprehending, and died of his wounds in Goal, as by a certificate from the County Court of Craven.

Committee of Claims

Morrise, a Slave

29 April 1762
William Peacock was allowed his Claim of fifty pounds being the valuation Mony of a Negroe Slave, to him belonging, called Morrise, who was burnt for Murder in Duplin County, as by certificate.

Committee of Claims

Tom, a Slave

29 April 1762
Mr. Andrew Knox Sheriff of Parquimans County was allowed his claim of four pounds for castrating a Negroe Man called Tom belonging to the Estate of James Long dece'd as p Acct. filed.

General Assembly Sessions Records 1709-1782

Committee of Claims

Jemmy, a Slave

13 November 1762
Thomas Jones was allowed his Claim of Sixty pounds, being the valuation Money, of a Negroe Man called Jemmy, to him belonging, who was tried by the Special Court in New Hanover County and executed for Felony at Wilmington, being the Second Offence, as p certificate filed.

Committee of Claims

Sambo, a Slave

13 November 1762
Lemuel Sawyer Sherif of Pasquotank was allowed his Claim of four pounds for castrating and curing a Negroe called Sambo belonging to Edward Williams as p Certificate filed.

Committee of Claims

Cesar, a Slave

13 November 1762
The Estate of James Parker was allowed twenty pounds for a Negroe Man named Cesar, who was executed for the Murder of his Master As p Certificate filed.

Committee of Claims
13 November 1762
Edward Rasor Sheriff of Bertie County was allowed three pounds for his trouble on the Trial and Execution of Cesar, a Negroe Man belonging to the Estate of James Parker who was executed for the Murder of his Master.

General Assembly Sessions Records
1709-1782

Committee of Claims

Dublin, a Slave

13 November 1762
It appears to your Committee, that in the year 1754 a Negroe Man called Dublin belonging to the Estate of Mr. Thomas Corprew, was executed for Murder, and valued at forty five pounds, which was never before claimed or allowed as p Certificate of Mr. Charles Blount.

Committee of Claims
13 November 1762
Benjamin Hart Coroner in Edgecomb County was allowed two pounds and eight pence for holding an Inquest over the body of John Hammond, who died drunk, & left no Estate.

Committee of Claims

Jemmy, a Slave

13 November 1762
John Walker Sheriff of New Hanover County was allowed his claim of five pounds one shilling and four pence, for castrating & executing a Negroe Man named Jemmy belonging to Mr. Thos. Jones, & his fees due on the same, as p Acct. filed.

Committee of Claims

Two Negroe Slaves

7 March 1764
Arthur Benning Sheriff of New Hanover County was allowed his claim of eight pounds for castrating and curing two Negroe Slaves, one belonging to John Duboise Esqr. And the other to Doctor Corbyn As p Acct. filed.

General Assembly Sessions Records
1709-1782

Committee of Claims

Joe, a Slave

7 March 1764
James Jeter of Onslow County was allowed his Claim of three pounds for nursing and feeding his Negroe Slave called Joe, who was castrated agreeable to the sentence of the Special Court of that County as p Acct. filed.

Committee of Claims
7 March 1764
Enoch Ward former Sheriff of Onslow County was allowed his Claim of twenty shillings for castrating a Negroe fellow belonging to James Jeter.

Committee of Claims

Titus, a Slave

7 March 1764
The Exors of John Daniel were allowed their Claim of Sixty pounds for a Negroe Fellow called Titus, who was outlawed and shot a p certificate from the Inferior Court of New Hanover County which is filed.

Committee of Claims

Dick, a Slave

7 March 1764
Hezekiah Russ of Anson County was allowed sixty pounds for his Negroe Slave called Dick hanged for poisoning a Negroe Fellow belonging to John Crawford as p Certificate from the Court filed.

Committee of Claims
7 March 1764

General Assembly Sessions Records
1709-1782

Bently Franklyn Deputy Sheriff of Anson County was allowed forty shillings for guarding and executing of Negroe Dick belonging to Hezekiah Russ as p Acct. filed.

Committee of Claims

Sam, a Slave

7 March 1764
John Simpson late Sheriff of Pitt County was allowed four pounds for castrating nursing & curing a Negroe Fellow called Sam, belonging to the Estate of Capt. Buck Dece'd, as p Acct. Filed.

North Carolina State Archives
General Assembly Sessions Records
November, 1766-November-December, 1768, Box #3

Committee of Claims

Rose, a Slave

6 November 1766
Matthew Raboun was allowed his claim of Fifty Pounds for a Negroe Woman Named Rose executed for House Burning in Hallifax County and Valued by the Court who tried her to that Sum as by Certificate filed.

Committee of Claims

Pompey, a Slave

6 November 1766
Richard Yates was allowed his Claim of Sixty Pounds for a Negroe man Named Pompey Executed in Hertford County for Felony and valued by the Court Who tried him to that Sum as by Certificate filed.

General Assembly Sessions Records
1709-1782

Committee of Claims
6 November 1766
Benjamin Wynns was allowed his Claim of Twenty Shillings for Acting as Clerk of the Court who tried the afore Named Negro Pompey

---

Committee of Claims
6 November 1766
John Baker Sheriff of Hertford County was allowed his Claim of forty Eight Shillings and Sixpence his fees for Imprisonment and Executing the afore said Negroe Pompey as by Account filed.

Committee of Claims

Luke, a Slave

6 November 1766
John Cherry was allowed his Claim of Eighty Pounds for a Negroe man Named Luke who was Executed in Beaufort County And Valued by the Court who tried him to that as by Certificate filed.

Committee of Claims
6 November 1766
Wyriot Ormand was Allowed his Claim of Twenty Shillings for Acting as Clerk to the Court who tried the aforesaid Negroe Luke.

Committee of Claims
6 November 1766
Roger Ormand Sheriff of Beaufort County was allowed his Claim of Forty Shillings for fees for Imprisonment & Executing the afore Said Negroe Luke as p Account Filed.

Committee of Claims

London, a Slave

General Assembly Sessions Records
1709-1782

6 November 1766
The Honble Lewis Henry De Rosset Esqr. was Allowed his Claim of Seventy five Pounds for a Negroe Man Named London who was Outlawed, apprehended afterwards and in Endeavouring to Escape was Drownded, as by Certificate from the Inferior Court of New Hanover County.

Committee of Claims

Toddy & Moses, Slaves

6 November 1766
Cullen Pollock Esqr. was Allowed his Claim of one hundred and twenty Pounds for two Negroe men Slaves named Toddy & Moses Executed in Bertie & valued to that Sum as by Certificate.

Committee of Claims

Simon, a Slave

6 November 1766
William Cray was Allowed twenty shillings his Claim for acting as Clerk on the Tryal of a Negroe man Named Simon belonging to Alexander Grant.

Committee of Claims
6 November 1766
Alexander Grant was allowed his Clain of Eighty Pounds for a Negroe Man Named Simon who was Executed in Onslow County and Valued to that sum as appears by Certificate from the Court who Tried him.

Committee of Claims
6 November 1766

General Assembly Sessions Records
1709-1782

Henry Rhodes Sheriff of Onslow County was Allowed his Claim of Eleven Pounds Eleven Shillings his fees for Guarding dieting & Executing a Negroe belonging to Alexander Grant as p Account filed.

Committee of Claims
6 November 1766
Samuel Ruffin Sheriff of Edgcomb County was allowed his Claim of one pound seventeen Shillings & four pence for imprisonment & executing a Negroe as p Account filed.

Committee of Claims
6 November 1766
Thomas Merret Goaler of Edgcomb was allowed his Claim of Sixteen Shillings & Eight pence his fees for imprisonment of the said Negroe as p Account filed.

Committee of Claims

Charles, a Slave

6 November 1766
Doctor Jacob Deadman was allowed his Claim of three Pounds for Castrating a Negroe Called Charles the property of Mr. Samuel Duncomb of Chowan County as p Certificate on Oath Filed.

Committee of Claims

Ben, a Slave

6 November 1766
Thomas Cook was allowed his Claim of Sixty Pounds for a Negroe Named Ben Executed in Bute County Valued to that Sum as by Certificate from the Court who Tried him.

General Assembly Sessions Records
1709-1782

Committee of Claims

Cato & Peter, Slaves

6 November 1766
Elizabeth Bonner Administratrix of Henry Bonner of Chowan County Deceased was Allowed her Claim of One Hundred & Sixty Pounds for two Negroes Named Cato & Peter Executed in Edenton and valued to that Sum as by Certificate from the Court who Tried them.

Committee of Claims
6 November 1766
Humphry Nicholls Sheriff of Bertie County was allowed a Claim of four Pounds for his fees for Executing two Negroes Moses & Toddy belonging to Cullen Pollock Esqr. as P Account filed.

Committee of Claims

Simon, a Slave

11 December 1767
William Cannon of Duplin County was allowed his Claim of Sixty Pounds for his Negroe Simon executed for the Murder of Lewis Bell as P. Certificate filed.

Committee of Claims
11 December 1767
James Sampson Clerk of Duplin County was allowed his Claim of two pounds for his fees on the Trial of said Negroe Simon as pr. Acct. filed.

Committee of Claims
11 December 1767
James Kenan Sheriff of Duplin County was allowed his Claim of three pounds for his fees and trouble in executing said Negroe Simon **[Torn]**

General Assembly Sessions Records
1709-1782

Committee of Claims

Boston, a Slave

11 December 1767
Richard Ward of Onslow County was allowed his Claim of eighty pounds for his Negro Boston executed for Felony and valued to that Sum as pr. Cert. Filed.

Committee of Claims
11 December 1767
William Cray Clerk of Onslow County was allowed his Claim of twenty Shillings for his Fees on Tryal of said Negroe Boston.

Committee of Claims
11 December 1767
Henry Rhodes Sheriff of Onslow County was allowed his Claim of four pounds for fees due on Tryal Execution of said Negroe Boston **[Torn]**

Committee of Claims

Dick, a Slave

11 December 1767
Thomas Edwards of Dobbs County was allowed his Claim of Sixty pounds for his Negroe Dick executed for Murder and valued to that sum as P Cert. Filed.

Committee of Claims
11 December 1767
Martin Caswell Clerk of Dobbs County was allowed his Claim of Twenty Shillings for his fees on Tryal of said Negroe Dick.

General Assembly Sessions Records 1709-1782

Committee of Claims

11 December 1767
John weaver Sheriff of Dobbs County was allowed his Claim of four pounds for his fees Trouble and expence in executing said Dick as P. Acct. filed.

Committee of Claims

Negroe Slave

11 December 1767
Francis Lock Sheriff of Rowan County Was allowed his Claim of Eighty pounds fourteen shillings for his fees guarding Sundry Felons and for Castrating a Negroe belonging to Elizabeth Flemming.

Committee of Claims

Bacchus, a Slave

11 December 1767
Martha Hill was allowed her Claim of Fifty Pounds for a Negroe man Named Bacchus Executed for a Rape in Bertie County and valued to that Sum a p certificate from the Court who tried him.

Committee of Claims

Cudjo, a Slave

11 December 1767
The Admr. Of Francis Corbin Esqr. Deceased was allowed a Claim of Eighty pounds for a Negroe man named Cudjo executed in Chowan County for Felony and Valued to that Sum as by Certificate from the Court who Tried him.

General Assembly Sessions Records
1709-1782

Committee of Claims

Quash, a Slave

11 December 1767
George Campbell was allowed Seventy Pounds for a Negroe Man named Quash Executed in Chowan County for Murder and Valued at that Sum as by Certificate from the Court who Tried him.

Committee of Claims

Jack, a Slave

21 November 1768
Ezekiel Moore is allowed Eighty Pounds for a Negroe Man Named Jack Executed in Halifax County for Felony as P Certificate from the Court who Tried him.

Committee of Claims

John Brown, a Slave

21 November 1768
Henry Ormond of Beaufort Coty. Is Allowed One Pound Eight Shillings and Eight Pence for Imprisoning maintaining and Releasing a Negro Man Named John Brown and Imprisoning Maintaining and Releasing a Negro Man Named Tom as p. Acct. filed.

Committee of Claims
21 November 1768
The Exrs. Of Saml. Thomas late of Northampton County Deceased are Allowed One Hundred & Sixty Pounds, for three Negroes who were Executed for Murder in No. Hampton County.

General Assembly Sessions Records
1709-1782

Committee of Claims

Robin, Jack & Jemmy, Slaves

21 November 1768
Howell Edmonds late Sher. Of Northampton County is Allowed Six Pounds for Executing three Negroes (To wit) Robin, Jack & Jemmy in sd County for Murder.

Committee of Claims
21 November 1768
Willie Jones of Northampton County is allowed Three Pounds for Acting as Clerk of a Special Court on the Tryal of three Negroes who were Exed. For Murder.

Committee of Claims

Phillis, a Slave

21 November 1768
The Honble. James Hasell Esqr. is Allowed Eighty Pounds for a Negro Woman Named Phillis who was run away and Outlaw'd Shot in taking and dyed of her Wounds.

Committee of Claims

Quamino, a Slave

21 November 1768
The Exr. And Exrs. Of John Duboise Deceased are Allowed Eighty Pounds Procl. Money for a Negro Named Quamino Executed in New Hanover County for Felony.

Committee of Claims

General Assembly Sessions Records 1709-1782

Slave, not named

21 November 1768
Willm. Salter of Bladen County is allowed Seventy five Pounds for a Negro Man Slave Executed in Bladen County for Felony, voucher filed with your Committee.

Committee of Claims

Will, a Slave

21 November 1768
Thomas D Vaughan Admr. Of Bryan Leers[?] is allowed Eighty Pounds for a Negro man Named Will, Executed in New Hanover County for Murder, Voucher Lodged with your Committee.

Committee of Claims

Johnney, a Slave

21 November 1768
James Hasell Junr. Esqr. is allowed Eighty pounds for a Negro man named Johnney Executed in New Hanover County Voucher filed wth. Committee.

Committee of Claims

Cudjoe, a Slave

21 November 1768
William Campbell Esqr. is allowed Eighty Pounds for a Negro Man Named Cudjoe who was Outlawed and Drown'd in Taking as P filed with your Committee.

General Assembly Sessions Records
1709-1782

Committee of Claims

Harry, a Slave

21 November 1768
Colo. Wilson Cary is Allowed a Claim of Eighty Pounds for a Negro Man Named Harry who was Executed for Felony in Chowan County as P Vouchers Lodged with your Committee.

Committee of Claims
21 November 1768
David Stanley Sher. Of Bertie County is allowed Five Pounds one shilling for the imprisonment and Subsistence of a Negro named Backus belonging to Martha Hill and other Services done in and about the Exc. Of the said Negro.

Committee of Claims
21 November 1768
Thomas Jones of Chowan County Clerk on the Tryal of Six Negros is Allowed Six Pounds as P Acct. filed and Lodged with your Committee.

Committee of Claims

Cato, a Slave

21 November 1768
Charles Bonfield Keeper of the Goal in Edenton is Allowed four Pounds Eighteen shillings for the Imprisonmt. Expences to the Guards to watch the sd Goal whilst a Negro Nam:d Cato was Imprisoned therein for Felony and finding wood to burn the said Negro as P Acct. and Vouchers Lodged with your Committee.

Committee of Claims
21 November 1768

General Assembly Sessions Records 1709-1782

Julius Nichols Sher of Bute County is allowed two Pounds for Expences paid for taking and Executing Sundry Negros as P Acct. & Lodged wth. Your Committee.

Committee of Claims
21 November 1768
Charles Jordan of Chowan Coty. Is allowed Eighty Pounds for a Negro Man Executed in the year one Thousand Seven hundred and Sixty five at Tarborough for Felony.

Petition
26 November 1768

To The Honourable The House of Burgesses Assembled and now Sitting at New Bern for the Dispatch of Public business.
  The Petition of John Clitherall of Newbern Mercht.[?]
Humbly Sheweth
  That on the 22d. January last Your Petitioner had a Valuable Negroe Slave Named Nero Stabed with a Knife at the Door of His Cabin in the Right time[?] by one Benjamine Parfett a Seaman who after having been in Custody for the said offence made his Escape
  The said Negroe Slave in a few days afterwards Viz on the 30th January Last Dyed of the Stab He received as above mentioned all which your Petitioner is ready to prove by Sufficient evidences and
  Therefore Humbly prays that He may be Allowed his Claim of the Value of the said Negroe
And as in Duty bound will ever pray.
Newern 26th Novr: 1768   John Clitherall
Evidences
Doctr Gaston
Richard Cogdell Esqr.
Richard Blackledge Esqr.

Craven County Ss.
Richard Blackledge Richard Cogdell And Dr. Alexander Gaston Appeared before me Jacob Blount One if His Majestys Justices of the

General Assembly Sessions Records
1709-1782

Peace for Said County And made Oath On the Holy Evangelist that they were Acquainted with the Negro Fellow Called Nero within Mentioned And that the Said Negro was Young & Likely, And reasonably Worth Eighty pounds or More money And That they believe he died of the Wound within Mentioned.

Richd Blackledge
R: Cogdell
Alxr Gaston

Sworn to before the }
26th of Novemr. 1768 }
Jacob Blount

****

North Carolina State Archives
General Assembly Sessions Records
November-December, 1768, Box #3
Committee of Claims

Nichols Sher
vs } Acct. The Public
£13.18.0

The Publick to Julius Nichols Sher. of Bute D	
To Expences Traveling to Capefare & back after	}£1.[Torn]
the two Negroes as book Goal	}
To procl. paid Capt. Mins for taking one Negro	2.0.0
To paid Chas. Burk for Going Out & back	}
after the Negroes	} 1.0.0
To my own Time Going Out & back	2.0.0
To Executing &C John Thorntons Negro fellow	2.0 [Torn]
To Executing William Williamsons Negro fellow	2.0.0
To paid the Gard Over the said Negroes while	}
in Goal after being Retaken	}1.0.0
To Capt. Ben Ward for taking Williamsons fellows	
the 8 Novr. 1768	2.10.0
	£13.18.0

This day Julius Nichols Swore before That he preformed the above Services According to law Certified under my hand this 8 Day of November 1768

General Assembly Sessions Records
1709-1782

Will Johnson JP

**Dvd. Standleys
Acct. agt the Publick
Allowed**

The Publick of North Carolina to David Standley Sher
1766 of Bertie County   Dr
To 61 Days Subsistence of Negro Baccus Slave
Belonging to Martha Hill for Felloney @ 1/   £3:1:0
To Goalers Fees for Commitment & Releasement   0:5:4
To fees foe Summoning a Court three different times
@ 13/4 Each   2:0:0
To Fees for Executing the same Fellon
November 4: 1768 Proved before me this Day
Cullen Pollok   (Seal)

****

**North Carolina State Archives
General Assembly Sessions Records
October-November, 1769; December, 1770-January 1771, Box #4
Joint Resolutions**

6 November 1769
Mr. Speaker & Gentlemen of the Assembly,
       This day was laid before this House a Claim of James Walker & Thomas Craig for a Negro wench outlawed and afterwards drown'd, which being disallowed by your Committee of Claims although Claims of the same kind have heretofore been allowed; We herewith send you the Certificate.

Granted to said Walker & Craig that you may Consider then of.
In the Upper House
By Order, J Burgwin Clk.

Slave, not named

General Assembly Sessions Records
1709-1782

26 January 1771
Message from the Govr. For Concurring with the Resolves for Mr. Howe
Mr Rutherford 1771 entd.
Mr Speaker and Gentlemen of the House of Assembly,
    I return You Your Resolves, One for allowing Robert Howe Esq Eighty pounds procl. For a Negro Man executed for Murder, The other for allowing Mr. Griffeth Rutherford Six pounds for shillings and six pence for the purpose mentioned therein, both concurred with.
Newbern 26 January 1771   Wm. Tryon

In the Assembly 26th January 1771
    Resolved that Robert Howe Esquire be allowed the sum of Eighty Pounds for a Negroe Man condemned and executed for Murder and appraised according to law.
R Caswell Speaker.

****

North Carolina State Archives
General Assembly Sessions Records
November-December, 1771, Box #5
Lower House Papers
Petitions Rejected or not Acted on.

Petition from the Inhabitants of Granville
1771, Entd.

To the Honble. the Speaker and Gentn. of the house of Assembly
    The Petition of the Inhabitants of Granville County Humbly Sheweth that by the Act of Assembly Concerning Tythables it is among other things enacted that all free Negroes & Mulato Women and all wives of free Negroes & Mulatoes are Declar'd Tythables & Chargeable for Defraying the Public County & Parish Leveys of this Province which Your Petitioners Humbly Conceive is highly derogatory of the Rights of Freeborn Subjects
    Your Petitioners therefore Pray that An Act may pass Exempting Such free Negroes & Mulatoe Women and all wives other than Slaves of free Negroes & Mulatoes from being Listed as Tythables & from Paying

General Assembly Sessions Records
1709-1782

any Public County or Parish Leveys and Your Petitioners Shall ever Pray &c.

John Smith, John Wilkerson, Charles Moore, James Norris, Christopher Thims, Thomas Head, William [?]ingson, John Head, James Caudill, Isom Caudill, Carter Hedge Beth, Martha Knight, Frances Davenport, Nathan Chiles, Benjamin Hendrick, Cutbird Hudjons, Willis Roberts, Isaac Head, James Williamson, Joseph Hill, William Thims[?], William Cawthon, Thos. Lowe, Wm Wallis, Isham Johnson, Isac White, Jno Tudor, Jno Badget, William Head, Groves Howard, George Fagans, Charles Spaulding, Henry Spaulding, Gibea Chavis, William Matthews, Benjamin Bass, James Downey, Richd Burton, Benjamin [?]aze, John Davis, Lewis Anderson, Davie Mircoll Negro[?], William Chavis, Samuel Huckaby, Lewis Collins, Thomas Butler, John Gwin, George Whitlock, Humphrey Davis, Josiah Stovall, Ben Bearden, Lovet Gates, Shadrach Roberts, Thomas Whittington[?], William Whorton, John Harris, Robert Downey, John Hart

      his   his   his
Edward X Bass   Rubin X Bass   Lawrence X Pettiford
    Mark   mark   mark
    his
Agula X Snelen
    Mark

****

North Carolina State Archives
General Assembly Sessions Records
December, 1770-January, 1771, Box #4
Joint Resolutions

Mr. Speaker and Gentlemen of the House of Assembly

       I am to request You will exempt Mr. Joseph Fulford, now upwards of Eighty Years of Age, from the payment of Public, Parochial and County Taxes. He has been a Resident in the Province since the Year 1705 (near Twenty Years before the Indians were last drove from Cape fear River) Served Seven Years in the War against the Indians between

General Assembly Sessions Records
1709-1782

the Years 1709 & 1719, and is at this present Time incapable of Labor; all which Circumstance make Him an Object of Your Indulgence. He is now an Inhabitant of Carteret County.
William Tryon
Newbern the 19. december 1770.

****

North Carolina State Archives
General Assembly Sessions Records
January-March, 1773, Box #6
Lower House Papers
Petitions not Acted on or Rejected

Pilot Petition, 1773

To his Excellency Josiah Martin Esquire Captain General Governor and Commander in Chief in and over the province of North Carolina
The Petition of the Legal Pilots of Oacock Barr Humbly Sheweth That your Petitioners under the Sanction of an Act of Assembly of this Province have Settled at Oacock Barr in order to attend and Carry on the Business of their Calling at Great Costs and Expence as well for the Benefit Resulting thereby as for the advantage of Mariners and Traders of the Province in General
Notwithstanding which Sundry Negroes as well free men as Slaves to a Considerable Number by unjust and unlawful means take upon themselves to pilot Vessels from Oacock Barr up the several Rivers to Bath edenton and Newbern and Bath again so the Said Barr to the great prejudice and Injury of Your Petitioners Contrary to Law and against the Policy of this Country and to Trade in General
Your Petitioners therefore humbly begg Leave to Observe to Your Excellency that the Pilotage at the said Barr at presents no ways answer the salitary Ends Intended by Law as Great Confusion and irregularity daily Insue from the Insolent and Turbelent disposition and behaviour of such Free Negroes and Slaves

Under those Circumstances Your Petitioners humbly pray Your Excellency would please take this Matter into Consideration And to

General Assembly Sessions Records
1709-1782

prevent the like for the Future by denying License or Branch to any such Free Negro or Slave Whatsoever

And Your Petitioners as in Duty Bound will Ever pray &c
John Williams, Geo Bell, John Bragg, Adam Gaskins, Richard Wade, William Styerin, Simon Hall

His Excellency's Message Respecting the Pilots
Petition of Ocacock Barr, 1773

I send herewith for your Consideration a Petition of the Pilots of Ocacock Barr, submitting it to your consideration, whether it may not be expedient to provide by Law for prevention of the Grievance of which they complain. As far as it depends on me I shall take care to obviate an evil that may be productive of the worst consequences to the Navigation of the several Ports of this Province to which Ocacock Inlet is the Key
New Bern February 24th 1773
Jo. Martin

****

North Carolina State Archives
General Assembly Sessions Records
March, 1774, Box #7
Lower House Papers
Petition-No Action Taken

Petition from Granville County, 21 March 1774

North Carolina Granville County September 15th 1773
To the Honble. Mr. Speaker and Gent. of the General Assembly

Your Petitioners the Inhabitants of this County think it our Duty to inform you that we suffer considerably in our Properties by Ill disposed Persons dealing with our Slaves in a Clandestine Manner. We Humbly apprehend that if a Law for that Purpose was enacted inflicting severe Penalties on the Violators thereof it might be attended with the desired Effect in putting a Stop to that pernicious Practice or we pray that some other Measure may be taken as your venerable Body shall think more Suitable to discourage so growing an Evil. That the Lord may direct and

General Assembly Sessions Records
1709-1782

assist you in all your Determinations so as they tend to promote his Glory and the Publick Good of this Province is the Prayers of

John Morgan, Lovet Gates, John Chambers, William Glover, Benjamin Bearden, Josie Stovall, William Williams, Thomas Head, George Norman, Robert Downey, John [Smudged], Richd. Head, Jonathan Knight, William Gragg, Nathan Chiles, John Dennis, Thornton Young, James McCallum, Rd. Thomes, William Giu[?], Benja. Whitehead, Joshua Nunn, Joseph Wade, Samuel Smith, Guy Smith, John Young, William Gra[?], Henry Graves, Richd Harris, Philip Yancey, Saml. Whitehead, Drury Allen, Wm Buckhanan, James Yancey, George Stovall, Henry Philip Hart, Ransom Boswell, William Owens, Hugh Galt, Hardy Crews, Saml. Pittard, George Newton, Joseph Willis, John Stovall, Saml. Jeter, Chas. Yancey, William Byars, Josiah Farmer, P. Pyles, Barthw. Stovall, John Rust, Thos. Reep[?], Thomas Yancey, Drury Stovall, Richard Duty, William Whitehead, William Allin, William Knight, Jesse Sanders, Isaac White, David Alen, Henry Spalding

****

North Carolina State Archives
General Assembly Sessions Records
November-December, 1777, Box #1
Joint Papers

A Message from the House of Commons, not concurring with the Resolve of this house in Selling the Negroes the property of Mr McKnight
Novr. 26 1777

State of North Carolina
    In the House of Commons 25th Novr. 1777
    Mr Speaker & Gentlemen of the Senate
        This House have received and considers Your Message informing that you have appointed Commissioners to Act Jointly with Commissioners already appointed on the part of the House to settle the public Accounts with John Wilcox relative to the Iron Works in Chatham County &c. &c. We also observe you recommend to the Consideration of this House whether it would not be more expedient to Sell the Negroes of

General Assembly Sessions Records
1709-1782

Thomas McKnight which have been hired there on Account of the Public than to hire them out as recommended by this House in former Message.

This House do not think it necessary to sell the Slaves of sd. McKnight at this Juncture and therefore would be excused from Concurring with in this Measure.

By Order John Hunt C.H.C.

****

North Carolina State Archives
General Assembly Sessions Records
November-December, 1777, Box #1
Joint Select Committee

Report of the Committee app'd to take into Consideration
the Memorial of Edge Tomlinson
Rejected

Report of the Committee for inquiring into the conduct of Alexander Gaston and William Tisdale esquires, upon the Memorial of John Edge Tomlinson

M Benbury Chairman -- M Maclaine Clerk
All the members present except Mr Person

Your Committee having before them the Persons accused, and the witnesses on both sides, proceeded to inquire into the truth of the allegations set forth in the memorial, and find that they are admitted to be true. The Justices in their justification or excuse alledge that M Tomlinson had treated his servant with great inhumanity for leaving his service, and that they did not think him safe in his possessions, unless he would give security that he would be forth-coming for him at Court, and until then, use him well; and at the same time they introduced the Clerk of Court with the minutes thereof, wherein it appeared that after Mr Tomlinson had refused giving security in the mode required, Mr Gaston had ordered the Indian into the care of Mr Tisdale until Court, and that the Court (present Alexander Gaston, William Bryan, Nathan Bryan, John Bryan, William Tisdale, Emanuel Simmons, William Randall and Andrew Blanchard, esquires) had offered to return Mr Tomlinson his

General Assembly Sessions Records
1709-1782

Servant he giving such security as Mr Gaston & Mr Tisdale had before required; and the trial was postponed to another term that Mr James Blount, who first purchased the Indian after his importation, might have time to produce some testimony to the Court

Your Committee find from uncontroverted testimony that his Excellency the Governor, John Cooke esquire attorney at law did upon being informed of Mr Tomlinson's complaint and the proceedings of the Justices, advise Mr Tisdale in whose possession the Indian then was, and before the County Court had taken cognizance of the matter, that the proceedings were illegal, and that Mr Gaston & Mr Tisdale had acted out of the line of their duty, and that it would be best for Mr Tisdale to return the Indian to Mr Tomlinson.

  Your Committee find that the act of assembly concerning servants and slaves, directs, in cases when any person demand freedom, that the magistrate before whom many claim of freedom shall be made shall
"cause the pretended owner of the person complaining together with such evidence, or evidences <u>as shall be material</u>, to appear before him, and after examination taken in writing, shall bind them over to the next County Court."
  Your Committee also find that Mr Gaston & Mr Tisdale, not only deprived Mr Tomlinson of his servant without any evidence whatever, but expressly contrary to the plain meaning of the act of assembly, and against the advice of gentlemen whom they must know to be competent Judges, and could not be supposed to be biased it appearing that Mr Cooke had declined accepting a fee from Mr Blount or being at all concerned in the dispute.
  Your Committee are of opinions that had no advice been given, it was the duty of Mr Gaston & Mr Tisdale to have asked it, at Court from those long acquaintance with our laws, and experience as magistrates qualified them to give such advice: Therefore
  Resolved by this Committee that the said Alexander Gaston & William Tisdale, as magistrates of Craven County have wantonly and against better information violates their duty as Magistrates, with intent, as appears to your Committee, to injure and oppress the memorialist and that their conduct renders them unworthy of acting in the respectable office of Magistrates.

General Assembly Sessions Records 1709-1782

Resolved that an execution of power without right, from whatever cause it proceeds, is oppressive to the people, and merits the severest censure of the laws; and that such exertion, particularly at this time, is pernicious and inflammatory, and tend to Disunite the good people of this State, and to drive them into measures against the cause of liberty.

Resolved that the clause in the Act of Assembly, here in before-in part recited, directing, that trials in cases of claims to freedom, shall be determined, by the County Courts, without any formal process of law, is of a dangerous tendency, and directly contrary to the 14th Section of the declaration of Rights; and that the said clause, and all other acts and clauses of the like nature, are inconsistent with our present happy constitution; for thereby a free man may be deprived of the principal part of his property, without a trial by Jury

All which is submitted
1st December 1777   Thos: Benbury   C: Committee

****

North Carolina State Archives
General Assembly Sessions Records
November-December, 1777, Box #1
House Joint Resolution

A Resolve of the Commrs. relative to the Iron Works, 24 Nov 1777

State of North Carolina
    In the House of Commons 22d Novr. 1777
On motion, Resolved, that Genl. Thomas Person, Mr Thomas Owen and Mr John Spicer be Commissioners on the part of this House to Act Jointly with such Gentlemen as shall be appointed by the Senate to settle the Account of the Public with John Wilcox relative to the Iron Works in Chatham County &c it having been left under the last Session of General Assembly; and also to hire out the Slaves that have been imployed on the said Works for or on Account of the Public.
By Order   John Hunt C.H.C.   A Nash S.C.
In the Senate November 22 1777
Read & Concurred With

****

General Assembly Sessions Records
1709-1782

North Carolina State Archives
General Assembly Sessions Records
November-December, 1777, Box #1
Senate Joint Resolution

Message from the Senate relative Jno. Montgomery
Resolve of the Senate Deciding James Miller to keep an Indian Boy as his Property
Dec 6 1777

State of North Carolina
     In the Senate 2 December 1777
On Motion Resolved, That Mr James Miller of Tryon County be directed to detain in his Possession an Indian Boy, taken Prisoner from the Cherokee Nation, which he now has, untill the Commissioners who shall be hereafter appointed by the General Assembly to treat with the said Nation shall otherwise direct.

Saml. Ash S.S.
In the House of Commons
4 Decr. 1777 Read & Concurred with By Order John Hunt C.H.C.

****

North Carolina State Archives
General Assembly Sessions Records
November-December, 1777, Box #1
Joint Papers, Petitions

The Petition of Alexr. Campbell for Consideration

To the Honorable the Speaker and Members of the General Assembly of North Carolina
     The Petition of Alexander Campbell Humbly Sheweth
That Your Petitioner came to This Country in 1775 With his family and A Few Servants, That at that Time Most of his Subject Lay in the West Indies, and Great Britain, that Understanding on his Coming Ashore At Wilmington That the Non Importation And Non Exportation Act was

General Assembly Sessions Records
1709-1782

soon to take place; he Applied to his good friend Cornelius Harnett Esqr., to Procure him Liberty from the Comitee of Wilmington to get in some Negroes of his, From St. Vincent, And Grenada, And as far as he recollects Mr Harnett was kind enough to Procure him that favor. That Accordingly he wrote by one of Mr Blackmons Vessels Bound to these places, for the Negroes: but that the troubles Increasing here, soon after, put a stop to him getting them in; Which Disappointment has made it Difficult for your Petitioner To Support his Family ever Since.

Your Petitioner is ready to Shew Vouchers, that his Principal Fortune lyes in these Countries, and that what he has here is but a very trifle.

Your Petitioner knows it as a real Certainty, that if he Woud sign the State Oath now offerd him, he Woud cut Himself out of every Shilling of his Fortune in these Countries Whether America, or Great Britain gets the Better in the Present War: For his Most immediate And Main Fortune at this time Lyes in the hands of Brothers in law of his in Jamaica, And they woud Undoubtedly make use of his Signing this Oath as a very Sufficient reason For Depriving him of his just Debts and Claim in That Island. As Your Petitioner is self Conscious [Faded] Of his own innocent And inoffensive behaviour since his Coming to America And Uninfluenced by Party work Pro, or Con, Since the troubles began (Which he hopes All his Acquaintances Will Vouch for him, as well as the Testimony given him by the Members of the Court of Cumberland) He begs the favor, and intreats the Honorable The Members of the Assembly Woud take his Singular And Distressed Case, Unto their Humane Consideration And if they shoud think proper to allow him to stay here to take care of his weak family, Untill there is peace Setled under the Sanction of their Laws, Or untill he Coud get a ship for the Grenadoes, or Jamaica, when & Where, he coud go with propriety for his Negroes &c. He woud get them good And Sufficient Security for his Quiet And peaceable Behaviour

And Your Petitioner as in duty Bound Shall ever pray &c.

****

North Carolina State Archives
General Assembly Sessions Records
April-May, 1777, Box #1
House Joint Resolutions

General Assembly Sessions Records
1709-1782

Slave, not Named

Message relative to Negroes Allowed for &c.

State of North Carolina
    In the House of Commons 30 Apr. 1777
The Committee appointed to inquire into the Claim of Thomas McLin for a negro Man Slave executed for Felony do report that it appears to your Committee by the Oath of Thomas Relfe that the said Negro was tried by a called Court for that purpose, Condemned and hanged first being Valued to Sixty five Pounds thirteen Shillings & four pence, your Committee are therefore of Opinion that Thomas McLin ought to be allowed for the Same as above mentioned
    The House taking the said Report into Consideration Concurred therewith
By order John Hunt C.H.C.   A Nash Speaker

In the Senate 5 May 1777
Read & Concurred with   By Order Jas.Granger C. S   Sam Ash S.S.

Slave, not named

State of North Carolina
    In the House of Commons 30 April 1777
The Committee to whom was referred the Claim of Robert Gibbs for a negroe Man Slave killed by Virtue of an Outlawry issued by Benjamin Parmela & William Russell Esqrs. the 4th Day of June last do report that it appears by the Oath of William Gibbs and Edward Spencer, that they knew the said Slave and that he was killed by Virtue of the said Outlawry, they further say on Oath that the said Slave was worth Eighty Pounds, it is therefore the Opinion of your Committee that the said Robert Gibbs ought to be allowed & paid the said Sum of Eighty Pounds for the said Slave all which is Humbly Submitted to the House.
    The House taking the said Report into Consideration Concurred therewith
By order
John Hunt C.H.C.   A   Nash
Speaker
In the Senate 5th May 1777, Read & Concurred with

General Assembly Sessions Records
1709-1782

By Order J.S. Gree[?] C.S. S.S. Saml. Ashe

The Report of the Committee appointed to enquire into the Claim of Robert Gibbs for a negro Man Killed
Concurred With
The Committee to whom was referred the Claim of Robert Gibbs for a Negroe Man Slave Killed by Virtue of an Outlawry issued by Benjamin Parmela & Wm Russlee Esqrs. the 4th day of June last do report that it appears by the Oath of William Gibbs and Edward Spencero that they know the said Slave, and that he was Killed by virtue of the said Outlawry, they further say on Oath that the said Slave was worth Eighty Pounds. It is therefore the opinion of your Committee that the said Robert Gibbs ought to be allowed and paid the said Sum of Eighty pounds for the said slave, all which is humbly submitted to the House.

Boatswain, a Slave

State of North Carolina
 In the House of Commons 30 April 1777
On Motion Resolved that Parker Quince be allowed the sum of Eighty Pounds for a Certain Negroe named Boatswain that was killed in consequence of an Outlawry, and that the Treasurers or either of them pay him the Same and be allowed in their Accounts, with the Public
 A Nash Speaker
By order John Hunt C.H.C.
In the Senate 5 May 1777
Read & Concurred with
Byy Order Jas Granger C.S. Sam Ashe S.S

State of North Carolina
 In the Senate 5 May 1777
Mr Speaker & Gentlemen of the House of Commons
 We herewith return three Resolves of your House for allowing Parker Quince, Thomas McLin, and Robert Gibbs, the Sums therein mentioned for Negroes Executed
Concurred with by this House Saml. Ash S.S.
By order Jas Granger C.S. Sent by the Assistant Clerk.

General Assembly Sessions Records
1709-1782

****

North Carolina State Archives
General Assembly Sessions Records
January-February, 1779, Box #1
House Joint Resolutions

Jim, a Slave

State of North Carolina
In the House of Commons 26 Jan. 1779
    Resolved that Mr Benjamin Clark of Bladen County be allowed the Sum of Eighty Pounds for a Negro fellow named Jim which was executed at Wilmington for Stealing; that the Treasurer or either of them pay him the same & be allowed
By Order John Hunt CHC   Thos: Benbury S:C
In Senate 27 Janr. 1779 Concurred with
By Order J. Sitgraves C.S

State of North Carolina
    In senate 27th Janr. 1779
Mr Speaker and Gentlemen of the House of Commons
Herewith you will receive the Resolve of your House in favour of Mr Benjamin Clark Concurred with.
By Order John Sitgraves C.S.   Allen Jones SS

State of North Carolina
    In the House of Commons 26 Janr. 1779
Mr Speaker & Gentlemen of the Senate
    We herewith send for your Concurrence a Resolve of this House allowing Mr Benjamin Clark a certain Sum therein mentioned
By Order John Hunt CHC
Thos Benbury S.C.

****

North Carolina State Archives
General Assembly Sessions Records

General Assembly Sessions Records
1709-1782

January-February, 1779, Box #1
Senate Joint Resolution

Mrs. Dupree £80 for a Negro, 1779
Message allowing Sarah Dupree a Sum therein mentioned
27 January 1779

State of North Carolina
    In Senate 27 Janr. 1779
Mr Speaker & Gentlemen of the House of Commons
    We herewith find for your Concurrence a resolve of this House allowing Mrs. Sarah Dupree a certain Sum therein mentioned
By Order J Sitgraves   Allen Jones SS

State of North Carolina
In the House of Commons 27 Janr. 1779
Mr Speaker & Gentlemen of the Senate
    We herewith return the Resolve of your House allowing Mrs. sarah Dupree the sum therein mentioned Concurred with
By Order John Hunt CHC Thos: Benbury S:C:

James, a Slave

State of North Carolina
    In Senate 27 Janr. 1779
Resolved that Mrs. Sarah Dupree of Brunswick County be allowed the Sum of Eighty pounds for a negro fellow named James who was Executed in Brunswick for the Murder of Henry Williams that the Treasurer or either of them pay her the same she allowed
By Order J Sitgraves C.S. Allen Jones SS
    In the House of Commons 27 Janr. 1779 Concurred with Thos: Benbury S:C:
By Order John Hunt CHC

****

North Carolina State Archives
General Assembly Sessions Records
January-February, 1781, Box # 1

General Assembly Sessions Records
1709-1782

House Joint Resolution

State of North Carolina

    In the House of Commons 6th Feby 1781
The General Assembly being informed that a suit has been instituted in the County Court of Bladen, by Original Attachment (Wherein Henry William Harrington is plaintiff and John Legget defendant) on sundry Negroes and other attached Estate lately claimed, and in the possession of the said John Legget, who having gone over to the enemy & taken Arms against the United States, and the said John Legget having Committed sundry Torts & Injuries on the property and possessions of the sd. Henry William Harrington it is but reasonable and just, that the Estate of the said John Legget should be subject and liable to make him satisfaction for the same, therefore
    Resolved that the Justices of the County Court of Bladen, be authorized, impowered, & required, to proceed in the said Suit, in the same manner as in other cases of Original Attachment, the act commonly called the Confiscation Act to the contrary notwithstanding.
By Order
    Thomas Benbury SC
J Hunt CHC

State of North Carolina
    In the H Commons 6th Feby. 1781
Mr Speaker & Gentlemen
    We herewith send for your Concurrence a Resolve of this House impowering and requiring the Justices of Bladen County to proceed in a suit Commenced in the Court of the sd County between Genl Harrington & John Legget in the Manner therein mentioned.
By Order
    Thos: Benbury SC
J Hunt CHC

H. J. Res. Feb. 6, 1781
---requiring Bladen County Court to proceed with suit between Henry William Harrington and John Legget (rejected)

****

General Assembly Sessions Records
1709-1782

North Carolina State Archives
General Assembly Sessions Records
June-July, 1781, Box #1
Senate Joint Resolution

To the Hon.ble Genl. Assembly of the State of N. Carolina now setting at Wake County Court House in said State

The Humble Petition of Philip Clapp of Guilford County in said State aforesaid ---- First would inform your honours that on the 27th of May last, your petr. being at home in the peace of God -- came Col. John Peasley of said Guilford County aforesaid, to your petitioners house, and did seize and bear off your petrs. negroes (to the amt. of five in numbers, to his own house where he the aforesaid Peasley now holds and detains your petrs. said property without law or right, and as your petr. has never had any day in Court either by Citation or otherwise nor has any legal orders ever been given for said property to be taken or Confiscated, and as a free born Citizen of this State your petr. does in the most Solemn manner Humbly beg, that your honours would take this matter under your Serious Consideration and lat him be heard on the premises, and order him his property again, or Grant reliefs, in any other way as in Yr. great Wisdom you may think for the best.

And Your petr. as in duty bound will ever pray.

Given under my hand at Guilford this 15th, day of June AD 1781
Philip Clapp

North Carolina
    In Senate 13 July 1781
Read the Petition of John Philip Clapp of Guilford County Praying &c. Whereupon

Resolved that Five Negroes the Property of John Philip Clapp of Guilford County now in the Possession or Care of the Commissioners of confiscated Property for the County aforesaid be restored to him the said Clapp, he first giving Bond with Sufficient Security to the Commissioners for the delivery of Said Negroes when called for by the Genl. Assembly.
by Order
    Alex: Martin SS

General Assembly Sessions Records
1709-1782

Jno. Haywood CS

North Carolina
    In Senate 14 July 1781
Mr Speaker &c.
    We send for concurrence a Resolve in favour of ------ Aldridge of Rowan; also a Resolve in favour of certain persons heretofore Citizens of this State therein described and likewise a Resolve in favour of John Philip Clapp of Guilford County.
By Order
Jno. Haywood CS

S. J. Res. July 13, 1781
-- in favor of John Philip Clapp (with petition) (Rejected)

****

North Carolina State Archives
General Assembly Sessions Records
April-May, 1782, Box #2
House Joint Resolution

Tartola Prince, a Slave

Order of the Court Rept. Tartola

State of North Carolina
    December Craven County Court 1781

The Court proceeded to value a Runaway Negroe belonging to William Bryan Esquire which was Killed by the Inhabitants of Core Creek, did Value the said Slave Named Tartola Prince to One Hundred Pounds Specie, It appearing to the Court that the said Slave and many others have Assembled and Committed many Acts of Felony to Suppress which the said Inhabitants Embodied **[Faded]** apprehend the said Out lying Slaves, the said Negroe was killed.
Copy
       Chrisr. Nealey C.C.

General Assembly Sessions Records
1709-1782

With Mr. Bryan's Resolve
1 May
Rejected

North Carolina
    In the House of Commons 1 May 1782
Mr Speaker & Gentlemen
    We send for Concurrence a Resolve allowing William Bryan Esquire of Craven County One hundred Pounds Specie

By Order
    Thos: Benbury SC
J. Hunt CHC

****

North Carolina State Archives
General Assembly Sessions Records
April-May, 1782, Box #2
House Joint Resolution

William Borden's Petition to the Assembly

To the honourable the General Assembly now sitting at Hillsborough
    The Petition of William Borden of Cartaret County, Humbly Sheweth
That Your Petitioner, has paid his public Taxes for the Year 1781, to the amount of 30000 Dollars and 200 Bushels of Grain

That by the late Incursion of the British Enemy into Cartaret County, Your Petitioner has been plundered and his Property destroyed in a very extra-ordinary Manner, (Viz)
Twenty nine Negroes carried off, two only are left, one of which is blind, the other very old, his dwelling House much damaged, the greatest part of his Household Furniture taken away or destroyed, his Saw Mill, Grist Mill, & Boulting Mill with a large Quantity of Plank burn't up, A Blacksmith's Shop & tools, a large Coopers Shop and Tools, with a Quantity of Barrels also burn't up, A valuable Sailing Boat taken away, a

General Assembly Sessions Records
1709-1782

Quantity of Naval Stores, spirits of Turpentine & Varnish destroyed or Carried away, All his Bonds Notes of Hand and other valuable Papers taken away Besides Cattle Hogs Sheep Poultry &c &c.

Your Petitioner begs leave to observe that altho he has Considerable Property in Lands, Stock and some hard Money, Yet by his sudden Heavy Losses he is at present unable to go on with any kind of Business -- He can do nothing in the Farming ways. He cannot carry on his Saltworks (for which he is now indebted 600 Bushels of Salt) and Negroes are not to be bought for Money

Your Petitioner therefore hopes this honourable House will think it no unreasonable Request when he Petitions for a Remission of Taxes, for the Years 1782 & 1783, And your Petitioner as in duty bound, shall ever Pray &c
April 29th 1782
    William Borden

Your Petitioner begs further to inform the House, that he hath a Letter handed to him by one of Beaufort Pilates from the Commanding Officer of the party that plundered him, Informing him that he hath all his Papers Consisting of Accompts Books Deeds, Patents, Bonds, Notes of Hands, and other papers of Consequence, which he shall detain unless he sends him Governor Martins papers which are in the Admiralty office in the Custody of William Tisdale, who thinks that those Papers were Delivered to him by virtue of his office, in Trust, and that he hath no Right to Give them up to any Person Except directed so to do, by order of his Superiors, Your Petitioner Supposes that the said Papers are of no Consequence to the State, and Requests that they May be Delivered to your Petitioner or his order that he may Exchange them for his own. And your Petitioner as in Duty bound shall ever Pray.
April 29th 1782
    William Borden

****

North Carolina State Archives
General Assembly Sessions Records
April-May, 1782, Box #1

General Assembly Sessions Records 1709-1782

House Joint Resolution

Jack, a Slave

State of North Carolina }3rd June 1781
Halifax County }

This certifies that at a Cald Court for the Tryal of Sundrie Negroes; Composed of the following persons (to Witt) John Justiss, Charles Pasteur, & Samuel Weldon Esqr. Justices & Augustine Willis, John Hargroe, Thomas Jackson & Abraham Johnston Freeholders & Owners of Slaves, that a Negroe Fellow, named Jack the property of Col. William Eaton Valued to Five pound Specie Charged with giving out Poison to several Negroes to Poison their Masters, was condemn'd to Die & Ordered to be executed immediately, and was executed Accordingly.

   Wm Wootten CC

Hannah, a Slave

State of N Carolina }
Halifax County }

This certifies that the Tryal of Sundry Negros, Composed of the Following persons (to Witt) John Justiss, Charles Pasteur & Samuel Weldon Esqrs Justices, & Augustine Willis, John Hargroe, Thomas Jackson, & Abraham Johnston, Freeholders & Owners of Slaves that a Negroe Wench named Hannah the property of John Green, Valued to One Hundred pound Specie, was Condemned to die and was immediately executed for endeavouring to Poison her Master
Witness my hand this 3rd Day July AD 1782
   Wm Wootten CC

North Carolina
  In the House of Commons 1 May 1782
Mr. Speaker & Gentlemen
  This accompanies two Resolves, the one allowing John Green a certain Sum therein mentioned, the other allowing William Eaton a certain Sum, which we send for Your Concurrence

General Assembly Sessions Records
1709-1782

By Order
    Thos: Benbury SC
J Hunt CHC

State of North Carolina
    In the House of Commons 1st May 1782
Resolved
    That John Green, of Halifax County be Allowed One Hundred pounds Specie for a negro Executed in said County
by Order
    Thos: Benbury SC
J Hunt CHC

State of North Carolina
    In the House of Commons 1st May 1782
Resolved
    That William Eaton Esqr. be allowed Five pounds Specie for a negro Executed in Halifax County
By order
    Thos: Benbury SC
J Hunt CHC

Consideration
Green, Eaton &c 1 May
Rejected

General Assembly Sessions Records
1783-1789

Chapter Two

General Assembly Sessions

1783 - 1789

North Carolina State Archives
General Assembly Sessions Records
April-May, 1783, Box #1
Senate Joint Resolution

>Miss Nancy Jones
>All.d £75 Specie
>In the House of Commons
>25 April 1783 read & Concurred with
>Edward Starkey Sp.
>By Order J Hunt CHC

I Genl. Ben Curry Collector of Port Roanoke, will take a receipt from the guardian of Miss Jones on this Resolve it will be received from him in Settlemt. of his Acct. Octo. 5, 1785
M. Hunt **[Frea?]**
by A. Paton

Andrew, a Slave

49

General Assembly Sessions Records
1783-1789

North Carolina
    In Senate 25th April 1783
read the Proceedings of a Court called in the County of Chowan for the Tryal of Negro Andrew the Property of Miss Nancy Jones, Whereupon
    Resolved, that the treasurers or within [?] of ther[?] into the hands of Miss Nancy Jones of Edenton, Orphan, or into the hands of such person as may be legally authorized to receive the same, the sum of seventy five pounds Specie, as a Compensation for a negro Slave named Andrew the property of the said Miss Jones, executed by public Authority, for which sum the Treasurer paying the same shall be allowed in the Settlement of his public accounts.

By Order
    R Caswell SP.
J Haywood CS

Received the above Sum of Seventy five pounds of Thomas Benbury Esqr.
L H Brewster Guard'n of Miss Ann Jones

****

North Carolina State Archives
General Assembly Sessions Records
April-May, 1783, Box #1
House Joint Resolution

                Wm Bryan all'd £50
In Senate 24th April 1783, Read & Concurred with
                R Caswell Sp.
           By Order, J Haywood CS

Slave, not named

To the Honourable the General Assembly
    The Memorial and Petition of William Bryan Sheweth, That Some Time in the Month of July in 1781 a negro man Slave belonging to your Memorialist Run Away and Joined himself with Sundry Other Out Lying Slaves and having Armed themselves with Guns &c, Committed

General Assembly Sessions Records
1783-1789

Several Feloneys and Attempted Sundry Murders in Consequence of which a party of Men went in Persuit of Said Outlying Rebel Slaves and in Indeavouring to Aprehend them your Memorialists Negro was Killed, he therefore Apprehended himself -- Intitled to Some Allowance for the Said Slave from his Country as the Act passed in 1741 in the 47 & [?4] Sections, Enacts, that if any number of Negroes or other Slaves that is to Say three or more Shall at any Time Thereafter Consult Advise or Conspire to Rebell or make Insurrection or Shall plott or Conspire the Murder of any person or persons Whatsoever Every Such Plotting Consulting or Conspiring shall be Adjudged and Deemed felony and the Slave or Slaves Convicted Thereof Shall Suffer Death, and that if in the Dispersing any unlawful Assembleys of Rebel Slaves or Conspirators or Seizing the Arms or Amunition of such as are by this Act prohibited to Keep the Same or in Apprehending Runaways &c any Slave Shall Hapen to be Killed or Destroyed -- The Court of the County where Such Slave Shall be Killed upon Application of the Owner of Such Slave and Due proof Thereof Made Shall put a Valuation in Proclm. Money upon Such Slave So Killed and Certify Such Valuation to the Next Session of Assembly that the said Assembly may Such Suitable Allown. Thereupon to the Master of Said Slave & Now May it please the Honl. Assy. All this your Memorialist has Obtained and Layed his Claim before the Last General Assembly which passed the House of Commons but was Rejected in the Senate for what Reason or upon what principles your Memorialist Knows not but presumes it hapned from the Hurry of Business being Late in the Session -- Your Petitioner, Therefore Hopes the Honbl. Assembly will be pleased to Reconsider the Matter and Grant him Such Allowance as they shall think Consistent with Justice and Your Petitioner will pray &c
      Wm Bryan

North Carolina
   In the House of Commons 23 April 1783
Resolved, that William Bryan of Craven County be allowed the Sum of fifty Pounds Specie for a Negro Man Slave killed in suppressing of Rebel Slaves, that the Treasurers or either of them pay him the same and be allowed in the Settlemt. of their Accounts.
By Order Edward Starkey Spr.
J Hunt CHC

General Assembly Sessions Records
1783-1789

No. 97, Claim all'd, £50

****

North Carolina State Archives
General Assembly Sessions Records
April-May, 1783, Box #1
House Joint Resolution

No. 150
Robert Jermain alld. £36,000
In Senate 23rd April 1783
Read & Concurred with
R Caswell Sp.
By Order
J Haywood CS

State of North Carolina
    In the House of Commons 23d April 1783
Resolved that Robert Jermain he allowed the sum of thirty Six thousand pounds or equivelent thereof in Gold or Silver in case the Currency cannot be procured for a certain negro fellow condemned by a Court called for the purpose of Trying him for the offence of Murder in Jones County and valued by the sd Court according to the directions of an Act of Assembly concerning the Trial of negro Hendr[?] & that the treasurers of this State or any of them pay him the same and be therefore allowed in the Settlement of their public Accounts
By Order
    Edward Starkey Spr.
J Hunt CHC
Rec'd from **[Faded]** Exum Esqr. Treasurer New Bern District forty five Pounds in Soliver in full and Ag**[Faded]** to the above Resolve
Robt. Jarman
June 1783

****

North Carolina State Archives

General Assembly Sessions Records
1783-1789

General Assembly Sessions Records
April-May, 1783, Box #2
House Bills

    The Petition of Thomas Hill, Joseph Cocke and Winifred Cocke

    To the Honorable the General Assembly of the State of North Carolina,
    The Petition of Thomas Hill guardian of Elizabeth Henry Hill, and Joseph Cocke and Winifred Cock his wife Humbly sheweth,

    That Henry Hill son to your petitioner Thomas Hill intermarried with your petitioner Winifred Cocke formerly Winifred Alston, and after having had by her the said Elizabeth Henry Hill died intestate: That your petitioner Joseph Cocke intermarried with your petitioner Winifred, and thereby became entitled in right of your petitioner Winifred to one third part of the lands which the said Henry Hill died seised of during the life of your petitioner Winifred for her dower to the said lands: That your petitioner Thomas Hill being desirous to advance and promote the interest of his said Ward Elizabeth Henry Hill proposed to your petitioners Joseph and Winifred, to give them out of the estate of the said Elizabeth, three negroes, to wit, Absey, Aggy and Elisha for your petitioners Winifred's right of Dower to the said lands, which your petitioners Joseph and Winifred are willing to attempt, and to relinquish to the said Elizabeth their said right of Dower, provided the title to the said negroes can be perfected to them; That as your petitioners conceive and are advised, this cannot be done, without your aid and interposition; They do therefore pray that you will take the premises under your consideration and make such ordinance or law as to your Honors shall seem right and just, and your petitioners as in duty bound shall ever pray &c.

    his
Thomas T Hill   Joseph Cocke   Winifred Cocke
    mark

****

North Carolina State Archives
General Assembly Sessions Records
April-June, 1784, Box #1

General Assembly Sessions Records
1783-1789

Joint Standing Committee

A Memorial to
the General Assembly
of No. Carolina

To the General Assembly of the State of No. Carolina,
    The Memorial of a standing Committee of the People called Quakers, Respectfully sheweth,

    That the Sovereignty of Conscience (we suppose) is acknowledged by the generality of Christendom to be the Prerogative of Almighty God, and that it is an indispensible Duty to keep a Conscience void of offence both towards Him and Men, and to do unto others as we desire to be done by; many among us, as a People, from a full and clear Conviction thereof, could not continue their fellow Men in Slavery, and transmit them from one Generation to another, as brute Beasts, apprehending the manumitting and setting them free, to be in no wise Inconsistant with the Principles of the present Constitution; and that it clearly Corresponds with a Declaration of the General Congress, which is in these words, "We hold these Truths to be self Evident, that all Men are Created equal; that they are endowed by their Creator with certain unalienable Rights, that among these, are Life, Liberty, and the pursuit of happiness; and that to secure these Rights, Governments are Instituted among Men, &c.

    No doubt, you are sensible that the freeing of Slaves is tolerated in several of the Northern States; and we believe many are lokking up to you, with desires that something may be done in favour of Liberty and Freedom: We therefore earnestly request, you may give your attention to these Important matters, and tolerate such as receive Liberty, to enjoy it.

    Sign'd on behalf, & by appointment of this sd. Committee in Perquimans County the 12th of the 9th month, 1783.

                          by Levi Munden, Clerk

The Commitee have appointed Joseph Henley & Benjamin Albertson to attend the Assembly, & present the above Memorial.

The Memorial of the People
called Quakers, April, 1784

General Assembly Sessions Records 1783-1789

Quakers Memorial In the House of Commons, 29 April, 1784 referred to Committee to resport on public dispatches.

The Memorial of the standing Committee of the People called Quakers. In the House of Commons 29 April 1784, read & referred to the Committee apptd. to report on the Governors Messages &c.
By Order J Hunt CHC
Read & referred as by the House of Commons
By Order Haywood CS

****

North Carolina State Archives
General Assembly Sessions Records
April-June, 1784, Box #1
Joint Senate Resolutions

Swift, a Slave

      Condemnation of Swift, the Property of Elijah Graves

State of No. Carolina Granville County Ss. At a calld Court to try a Negroe fellow named Swift the property of Elijah Graves, held at Granville Courthouse on Monday the 16th of June A.D. 1783.

Present: Samuel Smith, John Young, Memucan Hunt, Lewis Yancey, Esquires & Justices & Howel Lewis, James Downey, Charles Yancey, James Yancey, Freeholders & Masters of Slaves.

Who proceeded to enquire into the Circumstances & matters relative to the said Negroe Swift who being charged with having murdered a negroe man Slave the property of Jonathan Knight, but the one charge not being Supported he was discharged. Then the sd. Negroe Swift being charged with feloniously having Stolen & carried away Sundry Goods & other Articles the property of Lewis Yancey Esqr. & the said Charge being made good against him to the Satisfaction of the sd. Court they then Proceeded to Pass Sentence & ordered the Sherif to hang the said Negroe by the neck until he was dead, to be executed on the Twenty fifth day Instant, and then the said Court Valued the aforesd. Negroe to be worth

General Assembly Sessions Records
1783-1789

one hundred & thirty three pounds Six Shillings & eight pence Specie which the said Graves ought to receive.
Teste Reuben Searcy CC

State of North Carolina
In the Hs. of Comn. 5 May 1784
   Resolved that Elijah Graves be allowed the sum of Sixty Six pounds thirteen Shillings as recompence for a Negroe Slave named Swift executed by the public Authority that the Treasurer or either of them pay him the same and be allowed in the settlement of their Accounts
Tho: Benbury SC, By Order J. Hunt CHC
In Senate 5 May 1784, By Order J Haywood CS
Read and Concurred with, R. Caswell, SP.

****

North Carolina State Archives
General Assembly Sessions Records
April-June, 1784, Box #2
Joint Senate Resolutions

Tony, a Slave

       Outlawry &c Joseph Locke

State of North Carolina }
Bladen County   }

   Whereas Complaint hath this Day Been Made to us the Subscribers two of the Justices of the Peace of the said County by Joseph Lock that a Negro Slave named Toney belonging to the said Joseph Lock hath Absented him self from his Master's Service, and are Lurking in woods Swamps and other obscure places Commiting many Acts of fellony. These are therefore in the name of the State to Command the Said Negro Slave Toney forthwith to Surrender himself and Return home to his Said master and we do also Require and Comand the Shiriff of the Said County to make Diligent Search and pursuit after the above mentioned Slave, and him having found to apprehend and Secure so that He may be Conveyed to his said Master or otherwise Discharged as the Law Directs and the

General Assembly Sessions Records
1783-1789

said Shiriff is hereby Impowered to Rase and take with him such Power of the County as he shall think fit for apprehending the said Slave and we do hereby vertue of an Act of Assembly of this State Concearning servants and Slaves Intimate and Declare of the said Negro Toney Doth Not Surrender him self and Return home Imidiately After the Publication of these Presents that any Person May Kill or Destroy the said Negro Slave by such Means as he or they may think fit with out accusations or Impeachment of any Crime or offence for so doing without Accuring any Pennalty or forfiture thereby given under our Hands and Seals this first Day May 1780 and in the forth year of Amarica's Independence.

Robt. Scott (Seal)
Thos. Brown (Seal)

The Memorial of Joseph Locke

To the Honble. the General Assembly humbly Sheweth That your Memorialist had a very valuable Negro fellow that runaway from him for several Months till the arrival of the British Troops in Wilmington and the Friends of the American Cause determined that no such should be lurking in the Woods for fear of giving intelligence &c. They persued the said Negro and shot and killed him to the great loss of your Memorialist, He being upwards of Sixty years of Age and the only Negro fellow he had. Therefore your Memorialist prays your Honble. Body will make him such satisfaction as in your wisdom you shall think meet and he as in duty bound will pray &c.

Joseph Locke

The Value of a Negroe fellow Tony

The State of North County }
Bladen County }

We the Subscribers being Call:d upon by Mr. Joseph Lock, to Value a Negroe Fellow Toney the Property of the said Joseph Lock; who was Run a Way from his sd: Master for Several Months; And Lay Lurking in the woods and Doing Mischief in the Neighbourhood; til at Length the Neighbours Imbody:d and Pursu:d the Sd. Negroe Toney till they Came a Cross him and he Striving to Make his Escape was Shot And kill:d which Negroe we the Freeholders in sd. County Doth upon Our Oaths Say was

General Assembly Sessions Records
1783-1789

worth one hundred and twenty Pounds Specie Given Under Our hands this 5 Day of Septr 1783

Danl. Campbell, Willm. Lucas, Basil Manly, Wm. Oliphant, Jno Brown, JP, Saml. Smith, JP, Thos: Brown, JP

In Senate 30 April, 1784   £60

****

North Carolina State Archives
General Assembly Sessions Records
April-June, 1784, Box #2
Joint Senate Resolutions

Tom, a Slave

Papers on which the Allowance to Mr Jordain for Negroes executed are founded. April 29th 1784

Executed, Jona. Jacocks, Sheriff

Bertie County }
No Ca.   }

In Court of Trials held at Windsor for Trials of Negro Tom property of Isaac Jordain on July 10th One thousand seven hundred & Eighty three, for Breaking open a Barn & Stealing thereout Corn the property of Mr. William Gray; Present Zedekiah Stone, Anthony Armisted, Thomas Collins Justices; Thomas Shehan, Josiah Smith, Thomas Whitmell Pugh, & John Smith Freeholders for said Trial, do Adjudge the said Negro Guilty of Felony & to suffer death on Thursday the 10th Inst. between the Hours of four & Nine by Hanging; We likewise Value the aforesaid Negro at One Hundred Pounds Specie; In Witness whereof we have hereunto set our hands & Seals this 10th July AD 1783
The Sheriff of Bertie County to Execute
Charles Hughes, Ck s. Ct
Frdk Stone (Seal), Thomas Collins (Seal), Thos Shehan (Seal), Josiah Smith (Seal), Thos Pugh (Seal), John Smith (Seal)

General Assembly Sessions Records
1783-1789

Bertie County }
No Ca.   }

Jacob, a Slave

In Court of Trial held at Windsor for Trial of Negro Jacob Property of William West, on July 19th One thousand seven hundred &Eighty three; for Breaking open a Barn & stealing Corn the property of Mr. William Gray; Present Zedekiah Stone, Anthony Armisted, Thomas Collins Justices, Thomas Shehan, Josiah Smith, Thomas Whitmill Pugh, & John Smith Freeholders for said Trial, do Adjudge the said Negro Guilty of Felony, & to suffer death on Thursday the 10th Instant between the hours of Four & Nine by Hanging; We likewise Value the aforesaid Negro at One Hundred & Twenty Pounds Specie; In Witness whereof we have hereunto set our Hands & Seals this 10th July 1783.
For the Sheriff of Bertie County to Execute
Chas. Hughs Ck S Ct.
Fredk Stone (Seal), Thomas Collins (Seal), Thos. Shehan (Seal), Josiah Smith (Seal), Thos. Pugh (Seal), John Smith (Seal).

****

North Carolina State Archives
General Assembly Sessions Records
April-June, 1784, Box #2
Joint Senate Resolutions

Papers on which the Allowances to Eaton & Green for Negroes executed are founded. April 29th, 1784

State of North Carolina } SS.
Halifax County   }
At a Called Court for the Tryal of Several Negroes the property of several persons on the third Day of June 1781.
Present: John Justice, Charles Pasteur, Samuel Weldon, Esquires Justices. Augustin Willis, John Hargroe, Thomas Jackson, Abraham Johnson, freeholders and Owners of Slaves, Who were Qualified and took their seats.

General Assembly Sessions Records 1783-1789

Jack, a Slave

A Negroe Man Named Jack the Property of Colo. William Eaton of Northampton County being brought before the Court Charged with Giving out poison to several Negroes in Order to poison several people was Valued to five pounds Specie.

Said Jack being Arraigned and the Witness's Sworn and Questioned It was the Opinion of the Court that he was Guilty of the Charge and it was the sentence of the Court that he be hanged by the Neck While he is Dead, Dead, Dead, and that the Sheriff execute him Immediately.
Wm Wooten CC

State of North Carolina }
Halifax County }
    At a Called Court for the Tryal of several Negroes the property of Several persons on the third day of June 1781.

Present: Charles Pasteur, John Justice, Samuel Weldon, Esquires Justices Augustin Willis, John Hargrove, Thomas Jackson, Abraham Johnson, Freeholders and Owners of Slaves who were Sworn & took their Seats.

One Negroe Woman Named Hannah the property of John Green Valued to One Hundred pounds Specie Charged with endeavouring to Poison her Master and Family, the Witness's being Sworn and Questioned, it was the Opinion of the Court that she was Guilty of the Charge and it was the sentance of the Court that she be hanged by the Neck till she is Dead, Dead, Dead, and that the Sheriff Execute her immediately.
William Wooten CC

These may Certify at the General Assembly held at Hillsborough in April & May 1782, a Certificate Signed by William Wooten as Clerk of a Court called for the Tryal of a Negro Slave the Property of William Eaton Esquire of Northampton County, Certifying the Condemnation of the Said Slave as also the Sum at which he was valued; And likewise a Certificate from said Wooten certifying in like manner, the Condemnation and Valuation of a Negro Slave the Property of Mr John Green, were presented to the Senate by the Clerk of the House of Commons, together

General Assembly Sessions Records
1783-1789

with Resolves of that Body allowing Mr Eaton & Mr Green a certain Sum each, in Consideration of Such Execution; which Resolves for reasons I do not know at this time recollect were rejected, & are with those Certificates, as I believe, in the House File of that Session, which is not now to come at.
Hillsborough 25th Apl. 1783
J Haywood CS

****

North Carolina State Archives
General Assembly Sessions Records
April-June, 1784, Box #2
Senate Joint Resolutions

Magistrates Court Record

In Senate
Papers on which are founded the Resolves in Favour of Philips, Savage, & Kindred, 27 April 1784

Jim, a Slave

At a Court held at the Court House in Tarbro. on Monday the 6th day of Oct. 1783 for the Tryal of a Molatto Lad named Jim Belonging to Lovelace Savage for the Murder of Ally Allen.

Present, Isaac Sessums, John Dolvin, Elias Fort, Robert Bignall & Solomon Sessums, Justices

George Lynch, Thomas Hodges, John Phillips & Jacob Sessums, Freeholders & owners of Slaves.

The Above sd. Jim, a Mollatto Slave was Condemn'd to be hanged, & the Court then proceeded to value the said Jim and are of opinion that he was worth eighty pounds Current money of the State of North Carolina, & I do hereby certify that the said Slave was executed agreeable to the Judgment of the Sd. Court on the 6th day of Oct. 1783
Joseph Speed CC

General Assembly Sessions Records 1783-1789

Slave, not named

At a Court of pleas and Quarter Sessions Holden for the County of Hertford in the State of North Carolina at the Court House in Winton on the 28th Day of May and in the Year of our Lord 1782

Whereas a Negro Man the property of John Kindred being Executed in the said County for Felony on the 26th Day of Aprill Last,

Ordered that the said John Kindred have a Certificate for the Sum of Eighty pounds Specie as an Allowance for the Valuation of the said Executed Slave, to be paid Agreable to the Act of Assembly in that Case made and provided.

Certify under my hand at Hertford County the 25th Day of May and in the Year of our Lord 1782.
Saml. Harrell Clerk Court

John Kindreds Certificate. One half to be allowed

I do hereby certify that Mr. Etheldred Phillips did agreeable to order of Edgecombe Court execute a Negro belonging to Lovelace Savage, given inder my hand this 5th April 1784
Joseph Speed C.P.T.

****

North Carolina State Archives
General Assembly Sessions Records
November, 1786-January, 1787, Box #2
Committee of Claims

Sam, A Slave

John Lindsay exhibited his Claim for the Value of a Negro Sam, the property of the said John condemned and executed agreeable to law and was allowed fifty pounds it being one half of the valuation laid on the said slave by the Court who passed Sentence against, for which sum a Warrant is to issue on the treasury.

General Assembly Sessions Records
1783-1789

Peter, a Slave

Moore Wright exhibited his claim for a Negro Peter, condemned and executed for the Murder of John Miller and Sarah Gold, and was allowed the sum of sixty three pounds thirteen Shillings and nine pence, and the Treasurer is directed to pay the same and shall be allowed in the settlement of his public accounts.

John Giddy, Sheriff of Halifax County exhibited his claim for prison fees and his Services in Executing a negro who was condemned by a Court for that purpose [?] and was allowed the sum of forty seven Pounds twelve Shillings and eight Pence as per Voucher No. 7 -- will appear which sum the Treasurer is directed to pay and shall be allowed the same in the settlement of his Public Accounts.

Sam, a Slave

John Giddy for maintaining a Negro Sam Convicted of Poisoning a Negroe Woman 13 days and for executing the said Negro agreeably to the decree of a Court for Trial of said Sam.

Simon, a Slave

Benjamin Hicks exhibited his claim for the Valuation of a Negroe man called Simon tried and Condemned by a Special Court for felonious Crimes and was executed in pursuance of the judgments of the Court and was allow'd the sum of fifty Pounds.

Lymus, a Slave

Samuel Clegg exhibited his claim for a Negro Man Named Lymus his property that was outlawed and Shot as appears by the Certificate wherein the said Negro was Outlawed and Killed and was Allowed the Sum of Seventy two Pounds ten Shillings which sum the Treasurer is directed to pay and shall be allowed the same in his Settlement with the Public.

****

General Assembly Sessions Records 1783-1789

North Carolina State Archives
General Assembly Sessions Records
November, 1786-January, 1787, Box #2
Joint Select Committee

Quaker Petition

North Carolina
    In the House of Commons 6 Decr 1786
Mr Speaker & Gentlemen
    We propose that the Petition of the People called Quakers, which at present stands referred to the Grand Committee be withdrawn from the said Committee, and be referred to a Joint Select Committee, & have for that purpose on our part appointed Mr Franklin, Mr Sawyer, Mr Spaight, Mr Bloodworth, Mr Bonds and Mr Gardner.
    We have added Mr James Robeson to the Committee to whom is referred the Petitions from the Counties of Washington, Sullivan and Greene   John B. Ashe S.C.
By Order, J Hunt Clk

North Carolina
    In Senate Decemr. 6th 1786
Mr Speaker and Gentlemen,
    We have received your Message relative to the Petition of the People called Quakers, which we agree to refer to a select Committee and have appointed Mr Harget, Mr Stone and Mr Clint[?], who will act with the Gentlemen by you named for that purpose.
Jams Coor SS
By Order, J Haywood CS

Report on Quakers Petition

North Carolina
    The Committee to whom was referred the Petition of the People called Quakers relative to the emancipation of Slaves, having taken the same under Consideration beg leave to Report.

General Assembly Sessions Records
1783-1789

That it is the opinion of your Committee that the emancipating Slaves is impolitic and dangerous to the peace and good Order of the State and the Community at large, therefore they have determined that the Prayer of this Petition aforesaid be rejected.
All which is Submitted
Harget Chm.

North Carolina
In Senate 7th Decr. 1786 Read and Concurred with
Jams Coor SS
By Order, J Haywood Clk

In H Com 8th Decr 1786, read and concurred with
John B. Ashe SC
By Order, J Hunt Clk

To the General Assembly of the State of North Carolina. The Petition of the People called Quakers, inhabitants of this State humbly Sheweth, that Your Petitioners being Deeply Affected under a Consideration of the Abject State of the poor Enslaved Negroes, And being Desirous to fulfill the Injunction of our Saviour, Do unto all Men as you would be done by, In giving them their Freedom, which we Apprehend to be the Natural Right of all Mankind, Are therefore Engaged under an Apprehension of Duty to Solicit you once more for their Enlargement, at least to make such Provision as may enable your Petitioners who are Conscientiously Scrupilous of holding mankind in a State of Bondage; to Liberate such as we are under their Care, without their being exposed to the Danger of being again Enslaved.

Restone Lamb, Job Bond, Phineas Lamb, Wm. Williams, Jacob Winslow, Wm. White, Francis White, Zachariah Lamb, Wm [?]elton, John Rudduck, John Hoggatt, Isaac Mendenhall, Samuel Pidgeon, Jonathan Wheeler, Thomas Kersey, Benjamin Mendenhall, Henry Thornbrough, Mordica Mendenhall, Joseph Hoggat, Moses Mendenhall, Tar[?] Johnson, John Rudduk Jr., Wm. Tomlinson, Samuel Tomlinson, Jesse Kersey, Matthew Coffin, Toms White, Jno. Laurence, Joshua Davis, Joshua Johnson, Jesse Hoggat, James Pendry, William Piggatt, Mordecai

General Assembly Sessions Records 1783-1789

Mendenhall, Aaron Hoggat, Thomas Peterson, Josiah Bundy, Joshua Moore, Cornelius Ratliff, Jonah Jordan, Caleb White, Thos Hollowell, Benjamin White, Elias Albertson, Joseph Wilson, Thomas Moore, Isaac Wilson, Amaus Griffin, Josiah Tomlinson, Daniel Kersey, John Mendenhall, Ralph Wright, John Mendenhall, Stephanas Hoggat, Richard Mendenhall, Moses Mendenhall, Walter Thornbrough, Moses Hoggat, Thos Thornbrough, Caleb Reece, Thomas White, Samuel Moore, Thomas Jordan, John Smith, Aaron Morris, Matthew Macy, Joseph Iddings, Jno. Talbot, Benjamin Iddings, John Howell, [Torn] Mills, [Torn] Hoggat, [Torn] [Next three names torn], [Torn] Hoggatt, [Torn] Mendenhall, [Torn] Haworth, [Torn] Mills, Hezekiah Sanders, Amos Mills, Philip Hamm, Jehu Wickersham, Joseph Pattison, Richard Tony, Thos. Elmore, Robart[?] Johnson, Richard Lundy, Nathan Pike, Amos Lundy, [Faded] Sanders, John Sanders, Isaac Williams, James Brown, Joseph Mendenhall, Thomas Marshill, Saml Schooley, William Pattison, Richard Beeson, David Sanders, Joel Sanders, Thomas Cook, William Gardner, Jehu Stewart, John Rich, John Rich Jr., Abraham Woodward, Enoch Harlan, John [Faded], John Mast, [Name Torn], Nathan Farlow, Jesse Davis, George Thornbrough, Robert Brattain, Thos Palin, Mordecai Morris, John Overman, Benjamin Pruhar[?], Christopher Nichols, Joseph Bundy, Joseph Morris, Thomas Morris, Mark Delon, Samuel Brothers, Caleb Trueblood, Phineas Nixon, John Modlin, James White, Samuel Charly, Thomas Hill, Edward Bond, William Beard, Jonathan Gifford, Abijah Jones, John Beals Jr., Robert Lamb, Daniel Worth, Benjamin Coffin, Joseph Macey, John Hodgson, Thomas Branson, Robert Hodgson, John Mills, Joseph Worth Junr., Henry Macey, Samuel Stanton, David Reynolds, [Torn] hamness[?], Areelous Elmore, Barnabas Coffin, Thomas Hodgson, Richard Beard, Isaac Jones, Aaron Coffin, Amos Kersey, Silas Worth, William Hoggat, William Chamness, Jeremiah Reynolds, Samuel Ozburn, Jesse Wilson, Job Worth, Aaron Frornigg[?], Joseph Hodgson, Jesse Wilson, John Winslow, William Henby, John Henby, Edward Tatlock, Obadiah Small Junr., Christopher Nicholson Junr., Joseph Morris, Onidas Overman, Samuel Newby, Ephraim Overman, Phineas H[Torn], Jesse Harvey, Timothy Ward, Samuel Bundy, Richard Ratliff, John Henby, Joseph Hill, Axom Ellison, Benjamin [Torn], Christopher [Torn], [Name Faded], Jacob Elliot, Wm. Hill, Zachariah [Torn], John Bailey, Aaron Hill Junr., Benjamin Stanton, Jacob Cannan, Daniel Ozburn, David Ozburn, John Worth, John [Torn],

General Assembly Sessions Records
1783-1789

Elihu [Torn], Obed [Torn], John [Torn], John [Torn], Samuel [Torn], James [Torn], Henry [Torn], James [Torn], Michael [Torn], Simeon Lamb, William Ozburn, Joseph Ozburn, Peter Ozburn, Enoch May, Tho. Thornbrough, Wm. Coffin, Tho. Thornbrough Junr., Wm. Stanley, Strangaman Stanley, Jacob Hunt, John Macy, Hezekiah [Torn], Wm. Baldwin, Paul Macy, Wm. Coffin Junr., Micajah Ferril, Tim Russill, Geo. Rail, Caleb Jesop, James Thornbrough, Reuben Bunker, Jesse Williams, Isaiah Hunt, Peter Dillon, James Johnson, Even Stephens, Silas Williams, Wm. Stanfield, Micajah Stanley, Asa Hunt, Abijah Coffin, Joshua Dicks, Nathan Hunt, Benja. Benboe, Jacob Rogers, Daniel Baldwin, David Macy, Solomon Hiatt, Richd. Williams, Aaron Mendenhall, Saml Stanley, Christr. Hiatt Junr., Benja. Johnson, Jesse Baldwin, Wm. Hunt, Jno. Sother[?], Jesse Evens, Jona. Hiatt, George Hodgson, Isaac Gardner, Tho. Hussey, Caleb Johnson, Matthias Williams, Asher Hiatt, Jos. Thornbrough, Eleazer Hunt, Micajah Macy, Stephen Springer, Tho. Macy, Benona Mils, Abram Cook, Gayer Starbuck[?], Jesse White, Charles Cannady, Timothy Macy, Allen Unthenk, Thomas White, William Hunt, Abner Hunt, Wm. Robinson, Robert McCoy, John Symons, Josiah Trueblood, Thos. Newby, Thomas Sa[Faded], B. Albertson, Joseph Henby, Exum Newby, Josiah White, Benjamin Arnold, Jacob Wilson, John Symons Junr., Richd. Jordan, Job Parker, Reuben Wilson, Nathan Parker, Zachariah Nixon, Hav[?] Morris Junr., James Morgan, Thomas Overman, George Metcalf, Gabriel Cosen, John Nixon, Demsey Bundy, Charles Overman, Joshua Albertson, Charles Morgan, Caleb Bundy, Nathan Morris, John Price, Jordan White, Jeremiah Gilbert, Jonathan Price, Jonathan Morris, James Overman, A[?]ra Symons, Nathan Bagly, Joseph Morris, Joshua Albertson.

****

North Carolina State Archives
General Assembly Sessions Records
November, 1786- January, 1787, Box #3
House Joint Resolutions

Petition of Christian McKenzie

Report in Consequence thereof declared, Mr Winslow

General Assembly Sessions Records
1783-1789

By J Hunt

C: Mackenzie
C: Younge
In Senate Dec. 20th 1786 Read & referred to Special Committee, the Members chosen on the part of this House are Mr Wynns, Mr Campbell
By Order, J Haywood CS

In H Comm 23 Decr 1786 referred to Mr Blount and Mr Long
By Order, J Hunt Clk

North Carolina
   To the Honorable the General Assembly of the State of North Carolina
   The Petition of Christian Mackenzie and Christian Yonge at present of New Hanover County Widows.
   Humbly Sheweth, That the said Petitioners arrived in this State in the Month of December last and brought with them between forty and fifty Slaves from the State of Georgia with an intention of settling them here.
   That many of the said Slaves are Natives of this Country and several others were purchased here by William Mackenzie formerly of Wilmington Merchant deceased (the husband of the said Christian Mackenzie and Father to the said Christian Yonge) who removed from hence in or about the Year One thousand seven hundred and Sixty three with his family and Effects.
   That on Your Petitioners arrival in this State they were under the Necessity of giving Bond and Security for the payment of duties on the importation of the said Slaves in the same manner and at the same rates as if the said Slaves had been imported for Sale.
   Your Petitioners therefore humbly pray, that your Honors will be pleased to order the said Bond to be cancelled or to give such other relief therein as to your Honors shall seem expedient. And Your Petitioners will pray &c.

Wilmington	}	C: Mackenzie
December 1st 1786	}	C: Yonge

General Assembly Sessions Records
1783-1789

North Carolina In H. Commons 5 Jany. 1787
On hearing the petition of Christian McKenzie and Christian Young setting forth that they have lately removed from the State of Georgia into this State and brought with them a Number of Negros not for sale but for the cultivation of their Plantation and farms and that they are charged with the payment of duties on the Value of said Negros and praying to be discharged therefrom And it appearing to this Assembly that the facts therein set forth are true.
Resolve therefore that the Collector of Port Brunswick shall be and he is hereby directed to release them from the payment of the said imports and from all Bonds given for the purpose of securing payment of the said duties.
John B. Ashe S.C.

In Senate 5th Jany. 1787
The foregoing Report was read and Concurred with.
Jams. Coors SS
By Order, J Haywood CS

M Kinzie & Young, Schooner Betsey, James Sma[?] Master of from Savannah, Decr. 13th 1785
Amt. Bond £39.2.2/2

****

North Carolina State Archives
General Assembly Sessions Records
November, 1786-January, 1787, Box #3
House Joint Resolutions

Claim of James Blount

Esther, a Slave

Your committee of Claims to whom was referred the Claim of James Blount.

General Assembly Sessions Records
1783-1789

On examining the premises they find that in April 1779 a Certain Negroe Woman called Esther the property of said Blount was tried and Condemn'd by a Court held for that purpose and was executed pursuant to the Judgment of said Court, which said Negroe was Valued by the Court to Eight Hundred Pounds as will appear by the Proceedings of the Court to which Your Committee beg leave to refer Your Hon'ble House.
All Which is Submitted
Robert Dukins CS
John B. Ashe
Allowed £40

Report of the Com. On the Claim of James Blount

A Resolve for £40 in Consequence of this report, Mr. Cabarrus
By J Hunt CHC

The House of Commons 29 Decr. 1786, Read & Concurred with.
John B. Ashe CS
By Order, J Hunt CHC

Recommitted
Report of the Com. Claims on the Claim of James Blount
Special Report

In H Com 6th Decr. 1786
The foregoing report being read was Recommitted
John B. Ashe CS
By Order, J Hunt CHC

In Senate 6th Decr. 1786 read and Recommitted
James Coor SS
By Order, J Haywood CS

Your Committee of Claims to whom was referr'd the Claim of James Blount, Report

General Assembly Sessions Records
1783-1789

That it appears to Your Committee from the several Circumstances they have been able to collect, and from the Situation of Mr. Creecy, that the Negro Woman Esther the property of the said James Blount was Condemned by a Special Court for attempting to poison Her Mistress, and that she was executed agreeably to the said Condemnation and order of the said Court.

Your Committee cannot conceive that the Court had a right to pass Judgment of death against the said Negro for an Attempt only, and are therefore of opinion the said Claim be Rejected.

All which is Submitted.
R Dickins CH

****

North Carolina State Archives
General Assembly Sessions Records
November, 1786-January, 1787, Box #3
House Joint Resolutions

The Report of the Comt. Of Claims on the Claim of Reuben Grant

A Resolve for £90 in Consequence of this Report del'd Reuben Grant himself, 11 Decr. 1786
By J Hunt, Clk.

Slave, not named

Your Committee of Claims to whom was referred the Claim of Reuben Grant, Report

That from the relation of Col. Mitchel, and a Certificate from William Cray it appears to Your Committee, that a Special Court was called and held in the Town of Swannsborough in the County of Onslow for the trial of a Certain Negro Slave, That the said Reuben Grant had a Negro man Condemned to be hanged by the said Court, and was executed in pursuance of the said Judgment, That the said Court Valued the said Negro to one hundred and fifty Pounds, That the Sheriff of said County was allowed by the said Court the sum of Twelve Pounds, and also allowed William Cray the sum of five Pounds for his services as Clerk to the Court aforesaid.

General Assembly Sessions Records 1783-1789

As Your Committee are of opinion that the Proceedings of the Court on the tryal of the said Negro have not been fully laid before them, thought it most proper to state such facts as come to their Knowledge to this Hon'ble House for a determination thereupon.
All which is Submitted.
R. Dickins CM

****

**North Carolina State Archives
General Assembly Sessions Records
November, 1786-January, 1787, Box #3
Senate Joint Resolutions**

The Petition & Memorial of John Rutherford on behalf of himself & his Brother & Sister Willm. Gordon Rutherford & Frances Menzies Widow.

In Senate the 29 Decr 1786 read and referred to Genl Rutherford, Mr Galespee & Mr Stokes.
By Order, J Haywood CS

In H Comm. 29 Decr 1786 referred on the part of this House to Mr Bloodworth, Mr McClaine, Mr McDowell & Mr Hooper.
By Order, J Hunt Clk

To the Honorable the General Assembly of the State of North Carolina,

The Petition & Memorial of John Rutherford on behalf of himself & his Brother & Sister Willm. Gordon Rutherford & Frances Menzies Widow, Humbly Sheweth,
 That Your Petitioners were entitled under a Decree of the Court of Chancery of North Carolina to Divers Slaves and other personal Estate, and to lands purchased for some of them with part thereof, the whole being vested in Thomas Rutherford & Henry Johnston in trust for your Petitioners; and that your Petitioners were also entitled under the Will of Jean Corbin late of New Hanover County widow deceased, to a considerable property consisting principally of Negro Slaves & some small parcels of land.

General Assembly Sessions Records
1783-1789

That the greatest part of the Negroe Slaves settled upon your Petitioners in trust by the Decree in Chancery, have been hired out by the Sheriff of New Hanover by order of the Court of that County (two of your Petitioners being at that time absent Minors, and the other a Widow without any Agent in this State, & both the said Trustees being then dead) and held, together with the profits thereof from your Petitioners; and tho' your Petitioners instituted a Suit against the said Sheriff for recovery thereof, they never could get the same determined.

That your Petitioners conceived that by some one or more act or acts of the Legislature, the Rights of Minors & others incapable of acting for themselves had been saved, and your Petitioner John Rutherford, as soon as he attained to full age, left Europe, (where he with his Brother & Sister had been sent before the War for their education) and returned to this Country in hopes to take possession of that property, which the Justice and Humanity of the Legislature had preserved for them.

That your Petitioners were not entitled to any property in right of their Father, the whole of what he possessed being vested in his Children by virtue of his Marriage Contract with their Mother; and Deprived of that property, they will be left unprovided for under the said Contract.

Your Petitioners submit their case to the Justice of the Legislature, and pray a speedy decision in the premises. And Your Petitioners as in Duty bound shall ever pray &C
Jno: Rutherford.

Archibald Maclaine maketh oath that to his own knowledge the facts contained in the above petition are true, & as causes for his belief he saith, that he was concerned in the suit in Chancery therein mentioned brought by John Murray Esqr: against the late John Rutherford Esqr., and that by a Decree, therein, part of the Estate of the said John Rutherford was decreed to the said John Murray, and the remaining part (including the Negroes above mentioned hired out by the Sheriff of New Hanover County) to the trustees above named for the use of the petitioners, in lieu of the Marriage Contract to which they were entitled in right of their Mother. The Deponent also saith that certain lands were purchased for them by Thomas Rutherford the surviving Trustee, and that they were entitled to certain lands and Negroes by the Will of Jean Corbin deceased, he the Deponent having been concerned for Edmund Corbin deceased,

General Assembly Sessions Records
1783-1789

who claimed part thereof, under a Marriage Settlement between Francis Corbin deceased & the said Jean Corbin.
A Maclaine
Sworn to at Fayetteville the 28th Decr. 1786 before me John Ingram J.P.

****

North Carolina State Archives
General Assembly Sessions Records
November, 1786-January, 1787, Box #4
Bill to Vest Title in Negroes, Rejected

A Bill to Vest the Title of Certain Negroes therein Mentioned in Mr Sanders Lancaster.

In the House of Commons 16 Decr 1786, rec'd by the House.

In the House of Commons 22 Decr. 1786 read the first time & was Rejected.
By Order, J Hunt Clk

To the Honorable, the General Assembly of the State of North Carolina
 The humble Petition of William Sanders Lancaster of Wayne County, Sheweth,
 That your Petitioners Father William Lancaster of Wayne County aforesaid, being one of the People Called Quakers and making a matter of Conscience the keeping or holding any Persons in Slavery, hath according to the Custom of some among the Society of People called Quakers, Manumitted a Certain Negroe Woman named Patience & her Children Sam, Selah, Rachel & Priss who are now going at large & under no control of your Petitioners Father or any of his Family, as your Petitioner humbly conceives, contrary to Law. And as your Petitioner hath been in his infancy at great Labour and Pains in raising the said Negroe, with flattering hopes that one day he might receive some advantage from the same by the Gift of his Father of some one or more of the said Negroes, and as Your said Petitioner is not so tied down by his religious principles (he having renounced Quakerism) He humbly prays that the Title of the aforesaid Negroes, may be vested in him by such mode as your Honors, in

General Assembly Sessions Records
1783-1789

your Wisdom shall think proper to Adopt. And your Petitioner shall ever Pray &C
Fayetteville, December 13th 1786
Wm Sanders Lancaster.

    A Bill to vest the title of Certain Negroes therein Mentioned in William Sanders Lancaster.
    Whereas it has been made appear to the satisfaction of this General Assembly that a certain William Lancaster of Wayne County being one of the People called Quakers making it a matter of Conscience the keeping or holding any person or persons in Slavery hath liberated and set free as far as in his power the following Negroes, to wit, Patience and her Children Sam, Selah, Rachel and Priss, and that the said Negroes are going about at large and under no Control -- And whereas William Sanders Lancaster son to the aforesaid William Lancaster hath Petitioned this General Assembly to have the Title of the said Negroes vested in him, as [?] is nothing but just that he shou'd be rewarded for the trouble and pains he has been at in raising the said Negroes -- And whereas the liberating of Slaves in manner herein before mentioned is productive of many Private and Public evils and ought not to be contenanced,
    Be it therefore enacted by the General Assembly of the State of North Carolina and it is hereby enacted by the Authority of the same, That from and after the passing of this Act the title of the said Negro Woman Patience and her Children Sam, Selah, Rachel and Priss is hereby declared to be fully Vested in the said William Lancaster his Heirs and Assigns for ever in as full and Ample Manner as if they had been given him by William his Father.

Wm. Sanders Lancaster, Bill in his favour Rejected
22 Decr 1786

****

North Carolina State Archives
General Assembly Sessions Records
November, 1786-January, 1787, Box #5
Senate Bills

General Assembly Sessions Records 1783-1789

A Bill to Emancipate Caesar formerly a Servant of Samuel Yeargan Decd. In Senate Dec 25th 1786, read the first time & passed.
By Order, J Haywood CS

In H Comm 25th December 1786, read the first time and passed.
By Order, J Hunt Clk
Mr Williams & Mr A Blount

In Senate 29 Decr 1786 read the second time and passed
By Order, J Haywood CS
Mr Martin & Mr Bl[?]

In H Comm 29 Decr 1786, read the second time and passed.
By Order, J Hunt Clk

Rhodes & Dickson
In Senate 2 Jany 1787 read the third time & passed
By Order, J Haywood CS

In H Comm 2 January 1787 read the third time passed and ordered to be Engrossed, By Order, J Hunt Clk

---

Warren County }
February 1786 }

    This is to Certify that the Bearer, Ceasar is by the Last Will and Testament of Samuel Yeargain Deceased who was the Owner of Sd. Slave, at his Decease set free and at his Own liberty for and During the Term of Fifty five Years After the Death of Ann Alston wife of Wm. Alston, and Daughter of the Sd. Deceased.
    I also Certify that the Last Will and Testament of the Sd. Yeargain has proved in Sd. Cty Court and Admitted to Record in my Office, and also that from the best Information we have Just reasons to Know that the Sd. Ann Alston is Dead.
    Given under my hand
M, Duke Johnson Clk NC

General Assembly Sessions Records
1783-1789

A Bill to Emancipate Caesar, formerly a Servant of Samuel Yeargan deceased.

Whereas by the last Will & Testament of Samuel Yeargan decd. Late of the County of Warren, he did devise in his said Will, that a certain negro man of his property, should after the death of his daughter Anne Alston, wife to William Alston of Chatham County be set free, for and during the full term of fifty five years, and whereas the said Anne being now dead, it is thoght Just & right, the said Last Will & Testament should be adhered to.

Be it therefore enacted by the General Assembly, that from & after the Passing of this act, that the aforesaid Caesar, shall & may be at his own Liberty for & during the term mentioned in his Masters Will, upon the same footing & under the same restrictions as other free Negroes, are intituled to in this State & shall be known & Called by the Name of Caesar [Smudged] Law to the Contrary Notwithstanding.

****

North Carolina State Archives
General Assembly Sessions Records
November-December, 1787, Box #1
Joint Papers

Thomas Harvey Petition

In Senate 22nd 1787 read and sent to the House of Commons
By Order, J Haywood CS

In the House of Commons 22 Nov. 1787 read & Rejected
By Order, J Hunt CHC
Skinner-go for information

The Record of the Court on the Tryal of the Negro within mentioned was del'd to Mr Jonathan Skinner 22 Novr. 1787.
By J Hunt CHC

General Assembly Sessions Records
1783-1789

Tonay, a Slave

To the Honorable the General Assembly of North Carolina
    The Petition of Thomas Harvey of Perquimans County, Most Humbly Sheweth,
    That in December last your Petitioner had a Negroe Man by the name of Tonay in the Town of Halifax which Negroe was charged with having committed a Robary for which he was tried by a Special Court, and the said negroe man Tonay was adjudged guilty by the said Court & sentenced to be Hanged which sentence was executed on the $13t^h$ day of Jany. 1787 by which means your Petitioner is Deprived of a part of Property contrary as he conceives to the Constitution Except your Honors will grant him an Adequate allowance for the said Slave, there being a Law at that time passed Repealing a former Law granting an Allowance in such cases, but perhaps not known to the Court at the time they passed sentence on the said Slave, Now your Petitioner humbly conceives that it never was the intention of the Legislature to pass any Law to injure the Citizens of this State or that would Violate the Constitution by which all our rights & Priviledges are Secured, he further begs leave to inform your Honors that at the time the Negroe was taken into custody by the Sheriff he was sold to a Certain Mr. James Powell (by a Mr. Hinchia Gilliam who was Authorised by your Petitioner to dispose of the Sd. Negroe) for the sum of one hundred & thirty five Pounds a part of which sum was paid but when the Negroe was taken Mr. Powell Refused paying the balance of the purchase Money Alledging that he ought not to loose the Negroe as the Crime was Committed before he bought him, the dispute then was left to Arbitration who Ordered the Person Acting for your Petitioner to refund the money by him Received and that the loss should be his, He therefore Humbly prays your Honors to grant him such sum for the said Slave as you in your Wisdom shall think Just and your Petitioner as in duty bound shall ever Pray.
Thomas Harvey
Perquimans County, November 1st 1787.

****

North Carolina State Archives
General Assembly Sessions Records

General Assembly Sessions Records
1783-1789

November-December, 1788, Box #1
Committee of Claims

Jamy, a Slave

Sarah Dupree exhibited her Claim for a Negroe Slave Jamy that was condemned and burnt for Murder in March 1778, agreeable to the order of the Special Court called for in the trial of said Slave and was allowed the Sum of Eighty Pounds as per Voucher filed. Rejected.

John Cains esq. Exhibited his claim for summoning a Special Court for the trial of a Negroe the property of Sarah Dupree apprehended for Murder (and Sentenced to be hanged) also for executing said Negroe agreeable to the Sentence of the said Court, And was allowed the sum of Five Pounds.

Limerick, a Slave

Thomas Johnston Late Sheriff of Onslow County exhibited his claim for summoning a Special Court for the trial of a Negroe man Limerick the property of Col. Grant, also Witness to give Testimony against said Slave, and for executing the said Negroe agreeable to the Sentence and order of said Court, And was allowed the sum of seven pounds eighteen shillings.

****

North Carolina State Archives
General Assembly Sessions Records
November-December, 1788, Box #2
Joint Select Committees

The Petition of Thomas Fitt & Henry Hill

In Senate 18th Nov. 1788 read & Referred to the Committee on the Petition of Joseph Lach[?] Esquire
By Order, J Haywood CS
Bloodworth

General Assembly Sessions Records
1783-1789

In the House of Commons 18 Nov 1788 read and refered as by the Senate
By Order, J Hunt CHC

The Petition of Henry Hill & Thomas Fitt
A Report in their favour was delivered Mr Fitt 23 Nov. 1788 by J Hunt

---

To the Honorable the General Assembly of the State of North Carolina, The Petition of Thomas Fitt and Henry Hill Sheweth
  That your Petitioners undertook and prosecuted a Voyage to the Coast of Africa about the Month of October 1786, at which time the duty on the importation of Slaves as well as other property was only two & one half P Cent on the original cost of such goods or Slaves; that during the absence of said Petitioners Ship on said Voyage, an Act of Assembly laid a duty of five pounds per head on all Slaves to be imported into this State, which Law was to have effect on the first of May 1787, In consequence of which additional duty your Petitioners are greatly injured, and have no Source of redress except by an application to Your Honorable Body -- Your Petitioners conceive that this Law being passed to have effect before ships that were on their Voyages could possibly return bears too near an affinity to an export facto Law, & therefore requires the interposition of this honorable Body to correct the rigour thereof.
  Your Petitioners in order to gratify in Some degree the demand required by the Public, are willing to pay to the Collector of Said Duties, at the rate of five P Cent on the original Cost of the Slaves so imported which is double the duty charged on the importation of any other Goods brought into this State. -- From this state of facts we Your Petitioners hope that Your honorable Body will take the premises under Your consideration, and afford such relief as in Your Wisdom may be found expedient, and we shall as in duty bound Pray &c
Thos. Fitt & Henry Hill

The Committee to whom the Petition of Henry Hill & Thomas Fitt was referred., Report
  That the said petitioners had at a Considerable expence & risque, fitted out a Ship to the Coast of Africa for a cargo of Slaves; That at the time the said Ship sailed, the duty on imported Slaves was no more than

General Assembly Sessions Records 1783-1789

two and a half P Cent; that after the sailing of the said Ship & before her return, the Law was passed increasing the duty on Slaves imported from Africa; and that the Petitioners ready to make every Compensation in their power, are willing to pay double the duty which was laid on Slaves at the time they commenced the said Voyage,

Your Committee are therefore Unanimously of Opinion that the said Petitioners on paying double the duty receivable on Slaves on the first day of October 1786, that is to say, on their paying five P Cent on the original Cost of the said Slaves, they be exonerated from payment of any other or further duty on the said Cargo of Slaves imported from Africa some time in May or June 1787; and that the Collector of the imports for Port Roanoke Govern himself with respect to the said Cargo of Slaves Accordingly. All of which is Submitted.
Thomas Person, 21 Nov. 1788

In the House of Commons 21 Nov 1788 read and concurred with
By Order, J Hunt CHC -- Jno. Sitgreaves, Spkl.

In Senate 22nd Novem. 1788, The foregoing report was read and Concurred with. By Order J Haywood CS -- Alexr. Martin SS.

Invoice of Eighty slaves imported in Ship Janet from the Coast of Africa for acct. & risque of Messrs. Hill and Fitt

	Gal.	
56 Slaves at 150 Rum	8300	
10 do at 130 do	1300	
10 do at 100 do	1000	
2 do at 115 do	230	
1 do at 90 do	90	
1 do at 80 do	80	
	11000 at 1/9 p Gal.	£962.10

Five per Cent on £962.10 is   £48.2.6
Windsor December 3rd 1788
Thomas Fitt
Edenton January 20th 1789 the above Invoice was sworn to before me according to Law, Michl. Payne

General Assembly Sessions Records
1783-1789

This Report entitles Genl Benbury to a credit for Three hundred & fifty Six pounds 17/6 £356.17/6 that being the balance of the amount of the negroe Entry alluded to as P his Return for 1787, after deducting the Sum of Forty eight pounds 2/6 -- £48.2.6 the amount of the duties [?] by this Report Fitz & Hill are liable for as P their Invoice.
J Haywood, Treas.

****

North Carolina State Archives
General Assembly Sessions Records
November-December, 1788, Box #3

To the Honourable the general Assembly of North Carolina,
The Humble Petition of Sundry the Inhabitants of Mecklenburg County Humbly Sheweth,
That whereas in the year 1781 several of your petitioners did inlist into the Service of South Carolina, in the Brigade commonly called the State Troops, Commanded by Brigadier Genl. Sumpter: for which Service your Petitioners were promised a Prime Negroe for each Man &c. That several of your Petitioners did draw said Negroes in consequence of said Inlistment and Service; which at that time were taken from the Disaffected Citizens of said State; for that Purpose, by Order of the Commanding Officer - And the General Assembly of South Carolina did since pass an Act Confirming the proceedings of said Commanding Officer; yet the Disaffected Citizens of that State from whom those Negroes were taken (that have since been Permitted to return) have Instituted Sundry Suites Against Your Petitioners for said Negroes in this State.
Your Petitioners therefore Humbly Prays Your Honours that a Law may be enacted Similar to that in South Carolina Confirming the Property of Sd. Negroes In your Petitioners; and putting an end to many vexatious Suits that have Arisen and May hereafter Arise.
And Your Petitioners as in duty bound shall ever pray.

General Assembly Sessions Records
1783-1789

Will Polk, John Gibbens, Geo Graham, John Gilespie, Andw. Walker, James [?] Senr., James Moor, Andrew Moor, David Moor, Joseph Moor, David Moore, William Blacke Junr., William Blacke Senr., John Grifee[?], Jeams Blalok, Thomas Black, David Hinson, John Stewart, John Migee, Jaimes Ol[?], Ezekiel Black, Robert Enoch, JA Martin, John [Faded], John Wylee, Thom. Burke, W. Alexander, Geo. Alexander, W. Smith, Adam Alexander, Isaac Alexander, John Mackey, Evan Alexander, Moses McWhorter, James McWhorter, Steven Blue, William McCane, John McCane, Hugh McCane, William Fishear, Pall Fishear, David Starns, Frederick Starns, Thomas Walker, Thos. LeKey, John Hughy, John Stevenson, John Welch, Matthew Rodgers, James Davis, James Wahole[?], Denis Tites, John McCamon, William McManey, John Davis, Adam Davis, Isral Davis, Israll Wahob, John Rodgers, James Lesley, Alxr. Carns, John Lathan, Owen McKorkel, James McElroy, [Name Faded], John McElroy, James Shannen, John Grahon, John Crye, James McKorkel, John Williams, James McCashlan, Charles Adams, David Abet, Andw. McCane, Frederick Fisher, Charels Fisher, Harmon Mires, Daniel Baver, Daniel Winchester, Darling Belk, Archd McKorkrl, James Belk, Robert LeKey, Robt. Orr, Daniel Carns, John Walker, Hugh McCane Senr., John Gordon, Eleazer [?], J Williams, James deter, Samuel Crow, [Name Faded], [Name Faded], John Downing, John [Faded], Thomas [Faded], John [Faded], John Howey, Jno Rea, Jacob Gray, Alexander Gray, Shared Gray, Joseph Stier, [Name Faded], Thomas Cason, Moses Craig, Moses Lawson, John Cochran, Thomas Cochran, Charles Finley, [Name Faded], [Name Faded], James Cry, William [?], [Name Faded], [Name Faded], John King, Robert [?], Thos Robeson, Noblious [?], Alexr Osborn, John [Faded], John [Faded], John Greers, Robert Ramsey, Ezek. Polk, [?] Houston, Robert Porter, Mat. McClure, Saml. McComb, Jn. Nelson, George Howey, Robt. Do[?], Will Legatt, Thomas Salter, Joseph Caryl, Michael Freeman, Alexr. Hodge, Alexander Cambell, Abraham Miller, Sampson Gray, Wm. Hutchison, Alexander Gray, James Orr, Thomas Hall, [Name Torn], [Name Torn], Ezek. Polk, James Reed, Hugh Parks, [?] Haggans, Jno McCulloh, Philip Wike, Danl. Berhan[?], Isaac Price, Ja. Connor, Jas Porter, Isaac Cook, Alexr Nelson, Thos. Polk, Wm Black, William Wesley, Jas. North, Chas. Alexander, James Houston, [Name Faded], Robert Lucky, David [?], Joshua Gordon, James Lowery, James Finley, John McNeely, Benjamin [?], Wm Rodgers, George McWhorter, John [?], Robart Younce, [?]

General Assembly Sessions Records
1783-1789

McWhorter, William Finley, James [Faded], Thomas White, Moses McWhorter, Hugh McCrary, [Name Faded], Hugh Forbas, [Name Faded], John McNelley, Joseph [?], John Forest, John Crye.

****

**North Carolina State Archives
General Assembly Sessions Records
November-December, 1789, Box #1
Committee of Claims**

No. 21. John Walker Exhibited his claim for a Negroe man outlawed, and killed agreeable to said outlawry in September 1780 and was allowed the sum of Eighty Pounds.

No. 35. Mrs. Sarah Dupree Exhibited her claim for a Negroe man, Executed by order of the County Court of Brunswick for Murder in March 1778, and was allowed the sum of Eighty Pounds it being the amount of said Negroes valuation.

Jack, a Slave

No. 53. Philip Reaford Sheriff of Johnston County, Exhibited his claim for hanging a Negroe man named Jack, condemned by a Court held in the County of Johnston for the crime of Horse Stealing, and was allowed the sum of five pounds.

****

**North Carolina State Archives
General Assembly Sessions Records
November-December, 1789, Box #1
Committee of Propositions & Grievances**

Galloway, a Slave

John Walker Petr.
In H Comm 26 Novr. 1789 referred to the Commt. Of Claims

General Assembly Sessions Records
1783-1789

By Order J Hunt, CHC

In Senate 27th Nov. 1789 read & referred as by the House of Commons
J Haywood CS

No. 21, John Walker alld. £80.0.0

The Honorable the General Assembly

The Pettition of John Walker of New Hanover sheweth -- that on the 10th May 1780 Your Pettitioner Outlaw'd a Negroe Man slave by name Gallaway the property of your Petitioner And that in consequence of which on the 20th Sepr. In the said year of 1780 the said Negroe Gallaway was Killed by William Player. And farther Your Pettitioner sheweth that the said Negroe Gallaway was a Valuable Tradesman & was vallued by Two Justices of the Peace in the County Afd. To One Hundred & Fifty Pounds or Specie -- the above is refered to Your Honorable Body to give him such Relief as the nature of his case requires, And Your Pettitioner as in Duty bound will ever Pray
Jno: Walker, Fayetteville 25th Novr. 1789

Outlaw for Negroe Golaway

State of North-Carolina }
New Hanover }

By James Gekie and John Moore Esquires, two of the Justices of the Peace for the County aforesaid;
To all whom these Presents shall come, Greeting:
Whereas Information hath been made to us by John Walker That certain Negro Slave named Golaway belonging to him is run away, and lies out lurking in Swamps, Woods, and other obscure Places, committing Injuries to the Inhabitants of this State:
These are therefore to require and command the said Negro Golaway forthwith to surrender Himself and return home to his said Master: We also require and command the Sheriff of the aforesaid County to take with him such Power as he shall think necessary, to search for, pursue, or apprehend the said run away Slave Golaway:

General Assembly Sessions Records 1783-1789

And further, it shall and may be made lawful for any Person or Persons whatsoever, to kill and destroy the said run away Slave Golaway by such Ways and Means as he or they shall think fit, without Accusation or Impeachment of any Crime for the same, pursuant to an Act of Assembly, in such Case made and provided.

Given under our hands and Seals, this 10th Day of May One Thousand Seven Hundred and Eighty, and in the 4th Year of our Independence.
Jas: Geckie & Jno Moore
Negroe Galaway was Kill'd Sepr. 20th 1780 by Wm Player.

We hereby Certifie that a negroe fellow called Galloway the Property of Major John Walker was shott & killed by Wm. Player some years since & we do think the said fellow Galloway was worth at least one Hundred & fifty pounds Specie in being a Valluable Tradesman
21st Novr. 1785
Jno. Moore JP
Thos. Tann[?] JP

****

North Carolina State Archives
General Assembly Sessions Records
November-December, 1789, Box #1
Committee of Claims

                        Petition of Sarah Dupre'

In Senate 24th Nov. 1789 read & referred to the Com. Of Claims.
By Order, J Haywood CS

In H Com 24 Novr 1789 referred as by the Senate
By Order, J Hunt CHC

To the Honble. The General Assembly of the State of North Carolina now sitting at Fayetteville,

General Assembly Sessions Records
1783-1789

The Petition of Sarah Dupre' of the County of Brunswick of the State afiresaid humbly Sheweth That in March 1778 Your Petitioner had a Negro Man slave tried, Condemned and Executed agreeable to Law. Was appraised by the Court who sat on his tryal to the sum of Eighty Pounds Proclamation Money as by a Copy of the proceedings of said Court annexed will more fully appear. That your Petitioner very shortly after the said Tryal Moved into the State of South Carolina where she resided untill more than a year ago, wch. Put it out of her Power to make proper application for, and obtain the sum (unequal as it is to the loss she sustained) allowed by the said Court. That as she has now returned to this State, Old and well advanced in years, as well as infirm in her Constitution, and thro' misfortunes is left with but barely sufficient to keep her above want, all wch. Considered will render the Eighty Pounds above mentioned doubly welcome to her at this time. She Therefore, confiding in the well known Justice and Humanity of your Respectable and Honourable body earnestly intreats that you will be pleased to direct that the said sum of Eighty Pounds aforesaid to wch. She conceives herself intitled may be paid into the hands of Mr. Lewis Dupre' who will see it safely delivered to her.

And your Petitioner as in duty Bound Shall ever Pray &c.
Sarah Dupre', Nov 5th 1788

Sarah Dupre', £80 allowed, Agreeable to the scale of depreciation which makes only £21.6.8

****

North Carolina State Archives
General Assembly Sessions Records
November-December, 1789, Box #3
House Bills

Be it known to all Men, that whereas a Certain Negro wench named Emelia hath paid to me & for me the sum of One hundred pounds Currency in Consideration of which I hereby give up for myself my Heirs, Executors & Administrators all right title & claim that I may or can have to her services and do hereby declare her to be free. Given under my hand this 18 day of May 1785 - Signed Robt. Schaw.
Signed in presence of John Rutherford and Isabel Chapman.

General Assembly Sessions Records
1783-1789

These Certify that the Instrument of writing on the other side under the signature of Robt. Schaw is an exact Copy from the original, said to be the hand writing of sd. Robt. Schaw.

In Testimony whereof I have hereunto sett my hand & affixed my seal notorial this twentieth day of October Anno Domini 1789.
William Tisdale Notary Public for the Town of Beaufort.

To the Honorable the General Assembly of North Carolina
  The humble Petition of Thomas Lovick Sheweth that your Petitioner having in his own Right a Negro Woman Named Betty Which I wish to liberate and set free from my Service, from the singular & Very particular attention of the Sd Betty to me in a Number of instances during my Illness, And duly considering that She is deservedly intitled to her Freedom from any further Servitude and Slavery.
  Your Petitioner therefore Humbly Prays that you will in your great Wisdom Pass an Act or Acts to Liberate and set free from my Service the Aforesd. Negro Woman Betty, & Your Petitioner Will Ever Pray, &c &c
Craven County} Thomas Lovick

To the Honorable the General Assembly of both Houses of the State of North Carolina

The Petition of Chaponel

Humbly Sheweth that he has a Molattoe Slave Girl the age of about three Years and a half, old. Your Petitioner having a Desire of having her Liberated and called by the Name of Lucie, therefore prays your Honor's to have an act of Assembly passed for that Purpose as in duty bound your Humble Petitioner will ever pray.
Chaponel

To the Honourable the General Assembly of the State of North Carolina,
  The Petition of Ephraim Knight of the County of Halifax, planter. Humbly sheweth that your Petitioner is the owner of two Malatto young men called Alexander and Richard who have been raised in his

General Assembly Sessions Records
1783-1789

family and being desirous that they may become usefull members of society and that they may participate in the blessings of a free Government humbly prays your Honors to pass an Act to establish their freedom by legislative authority.

And your Petitioner as in duty bound shall ever pray &c

Epm. Knight

To the Honobl. The General Assembly of the State of North Carolina, now Sitting at Fayette Ville.

The Petition of Thomas Newman Humbly sheweth, that he has a molatto Boy about two or three years old, and your Petitioner being about to leave this State, he is desirous to liberate and aet the said Boy free, and have him Called and known by the Name of Thomas, Your Petitioner therefore requests Your Honbl. Body to Pass an act of Assembly for that purpose, & your Petitioner as in duty bound will ever pray.

Thomas Newman, Fayette Ville, Decr. 2d 1789

A Bill to emancipate certain Negroes therein mentioned.

Whereas it hath been represented to this General Assembly that Robert Schaw in his life time did receive a valuable consideration for the further services of a certain Negro woman named Amelia and has certified the same, and declared her to be free. And by the Petition of Thomas Lovick it appears to be his desire that a certain Negro Woman by the name of Betty belonging to him should be set free. Also a petition of Monsieur Chaponel desiring to have set free a Mulatto slave belonging to him by the name of Lucy of three and half years old.

Be it therefore enacted by the General Assembly of the State of North Carolina and it is hereby enacted by the authority of the same, that the Negro woman called Amelia and the Negro woman Betty and also the mulatto Girl Lucy, Shall be and are hereby declared to be emancipated and set free to all intents & purposes, and shall be entitled to all the previleges and benefits of freedom in as full and ample manner as if they had been born free.

General Assembly Sessions Records
1783-1789

A Bill to emancipate certain Negroes therein mentioned.

In Hcom 12th Novr 1789 read the first time & passed
By Order, J Hunt CHC
Mr Wood & Mr Gillispie

In Senate 14 Nov 1789 read the first time & passed.
By Order J Haywood CS

In Hcom 3d Decr 1789 read the 2d time amended & passed.
By Order J Hunt CHC
Mr Guion, Mr Chisson & Mr McKay

In Senate 11th Decem. 1789 read the second time and passed.
J Haywood CS
Mr Wynns

In House of Commons 16 Decr 1789 read the third time ammended and passed
By Order, J Hunt CHC
Mr Johnston & Mr Alderson

In Senate 17th Decr 1789 read the third time, passed & Ordered to be Engrossed
J Haywood CS

And whereas it appears by the Petition of Ephraim Knight of Halifax County that he is desirous to emancipate two young Malatto men called Richard and Alexander the property of said Ephraim and it hath also been represented to this Assembly by John Alderson of Hyde County that it is his desire to set free a Malatto Boy belonging to him called Sam. **[Editor's Note: The rest of this document is missing.]**

And whereas it hath been made to appear to this Assembly by the Petition of Thomas Newman of Fayette Ville, that he hath a Molatto Boy belonging to him which he is desirous to emancipate, and known by the Name of Thomas Clinch.

General Assembly Sessions Records
1783-1789

Be it enacted by the General Assembly of the State of North Carolina and it is hereby enacted by the authority of the same that the said Negroe Women called Amelia and Betty and the malatto girl Lucy, and the said Malatto men Richard and Alexander and the said Malatto boy called Sam & the negro boy named Thomas Clinch shall be and they and each of them are hereby emancipated and declared free and the said Richard and Alexander shall take and use the surname of Day, and the molatto boy Sam shall be known and called by the name of Samuel Johns-son and the said Slaves so liberated and each of them are hereby declared to be able and capable in Law to possess and enjoy every right priviledge and immunity in as full and ample manner as the could or might have done if they had been born free.

Chapter Three

Secretary of State Papers

Magistrates Courts

North Carolina State Archives
Magistrates and Freeholders Courts, 1715-1793
Secretary of State Papers, Box #311

[Editor's Note: This description was included in the box containing the original trial manuscripts. It was undoubtedly authored by someone from the North Carolina State Archives.]

Magistrates and Freeholders Courts were special or called courts erected to try slaves under provisions of the following acts: **1715 NC c.66, s.11; 1720 NC c.5; 1741 NC c.24, s.46-55; and II 1764 NC c.8, s.3** Jurisdiction of the court, which was comprised of three of the county magistrates and four freeholders who were slave owners in the county where the slave's crime took place, extended to life and limb and was final, though speedy exercise of the writ of certiorari could prevent execution of sentence until the trial had been reviewed by the district superior court.

Records of these courts may exist in three forms: **(1)** a transcription of the proceedings in the trial; **(2)** writs and depositions of witnesses; and **(3)** certification of execution of the death sentence which

Secretary of State Papers
Magistrates Courts

was forwarded to the General Assembly's committee of claims in order to effect monetary compensation to the owner of the executed slave. Records, when still in existence may be found among county records, district superior court records, secretary of state's records, records of the treasurer and comptroller, or records of the governor's office.

Among county records, transcriptions of proceedings of slave trials can sometimes be found copied into the volumes containing minutes of the court of pleas and quarter sessions. Loose transcriptions and depositions in the cases may sometimes be found described and filed among the miscellaneous county records.

Some additional locations of transcriptions of proceedings of magistrates and freeholders courts for the trial of slaves, and certifications of the execution of the sentence of death, are:

District Halifax Superior Court. Miscellaneous Records, **1763-1808**.

Includes both transcriptions of proceedings and certifications of execution during the years from **1765 to 1774**.

New Bern District Superior Court. Miscellaneous Records, **1758-1806**.

Includes transcriptions of proceedings in two trials, one in **1775** and one in **1799**.

Secretary of State. Court Records. Magistrates and Freeholders Courts.

Includes transcriptions of proceedings and certifications of execution during the years from **1740** through **1786**.

Treasurer and Comptroller. Miscellaneous Group **(1738-1909). (Box 8)**.

Includes transcriptions of proceedings, certifications of execution, and warrants for compensation, for the years from **1738** through **1798**.

Miscellaneous Collections, Slavery Papers, **1747-1850**.

This artificial collection of materials was formed at some unknown time in the recent past from various groups of records. It includes transcriptions of proceedings from four trials held between 1748 and **1786**.

Governor's Office. Committee of Claims Reports, **1754-1764**.

These two volumes include the record of compensation allowed by the General Assembly's committee on the basis of certifications of execution described above.

Legislative Papers, **1757-1762 (L.P. 2)**.

Includes the transcription of proceedings of a **1759** trial which should have formed part of the records of the Assembly's committee of

Secretary of State Papers
Magistrates Courts

claims, but which become mixed with the regular records of the legislature.

Magistrates and freeholders courts ceased when jurisdiction for trials of slaves was transferred to the county courts of pleas and quarter sessions under provisions of **1793 NC c.5.** Jurisdiction was further altered when felonies extending to life and limb and clergiable felonies were placed under the exclusive jurisdiction of the county superior courts by the acts **1816 NC c.14 and 1825 NC c. 24.**

****

North Carolina State Archives
Magistrates and Freeholders Courts, 1715-1793
Secretary of State Papers, Box #311

Scipio, a Slave

North Carolina   }
Pasquotank County   }

The Tryall Examination and Condemnation of a Negro man Slave called Scipio at a Special Court called and hold the 22nd day of February anno Dom 1741, the property of Mr. Bartholomew Evans for felony and Burglary.

Present the Worshipful
Thomas Hunter
James George
David George
Esqrs: Justices

Gentleman
Thomas Pendleton
Symon Bryan
Thomas Woodby
Oliver Salter
Freeholders

Secretary of State Papers
Magistrates Courts

That the afsaid Negro Scipio on the Eighteenth day of February in the night time on the plantation of Mrs: William Turner in the County Afsd. the storehouse of Mr. James Gregory merchant on the said plantation broke open and there Feloniously did take & carry away Sundry dry goods the property of the said James Gregory to the Value of Two hundred pounds Currt. Bills of North Carolina. Then the Afsd Mr. James Gregory being called declared upon the holy Evangelist that on the 18th day of February in the year afsaid in the night time his storehouse was broak open & Sundry sorts of Dry goods was taken away to the Value of two hundred pounds. The afsaid Negro Scipio being called and Examined concerning the premises and Confest he broak open the store house and took away the goods, and returned them to the said James Gregory.
[Torn] & Freeholders

It was Further Considered by the afsaid Magistrates & Freeholders that the said Bartholomew Evans be paid by the Publick the Sum Twenty Nine Pounds Seven Shillings Proclamation money for the said Negro Scipio Given under our hands & Seals the 13th day of April anno Dom 1742.

Thos. Hunter, James George, David George, Thos. Pendleton, Thomas [Smeared], Simon Bryan, Olivr. Saltar.

The Within Claim was allowed April 2d. 1743.

****

North Carolina State Archives
Magistrates and Freeholders Courts, 1715-1793
Secretary of State Papers, Box #311

Phill, a Slave

North Carolina }
Craven County   }

At a Special Sessions began & held at the Court house in New Bern on the 18th day of November anno Dom 1743

Secretary of State Papers
Magistrates Courts

Present Justices
John Powel
John Bryan
Frances Stringer

freeholders
Walter Lane
George Bould
Robert Jarman
Jonathan Bangs

After the Proclamation made the freeholders Solemnly Called appears & was Qualifyed accordingly took there places.

A Negro Man Belonging to George Scipper Named Phill was arraigned at the Barr for a Rape Committed on the body of Sarah Baucum Wife of Nicholas Baucum and being Examined by John Powel Esqr. Eldest in Co[?] upon the Bench the Prisoner Confessed the fact. John Powel Esqr being desired by his fellow Justices & freeholders assistants to prove upon oath what Relation the [Torn] want of Paper could not committed to writing how & Concerning the Rape Committed on her body by the sd. negro Phill who declared upon oath that she said he the sd Negro actually committed the Rape aforesd upon her body.

The question being put whether the Confession with the womans Deposison be Sufficient to Convict him, which was carryed by the Whole Bench that it is Sufficient therefore accordingly he is found Guilty of the fact.

The Judgment awarded is that the prisoner at the Bar be Hanged till he is dead & then his private parts Cut off & thrown in his face on the nineteenth day of nov[?]

The Valuation Set upon the sd. Negro Phill is Thirty pounds Proclamation Money Ordr. a Certificate be made out

Mr Lane, Frs. Stringer, J Powel, Rob Jarman, Gorge Bould, Jonathan Bangs, & John Bryan

Secretary of State Papers
Magistrates Courts

****

North Carolina State Archives
Magistrates and Freeholders Courts, 1715-1793
Secretary of State Papers, Box #311

Josey, a Slave

> Job Howes Petition To the Committee
> of Claims
>
> The within Claim Allowed
> 27th November 1744

To the Worshipfull Chairman & the rest of the Gentlemen of the Comittee for Examining and Allowing Publick Claims

    The Petition & Remonstrance of Job Howes Humbly Sheweth that Your Petitioner had a Certain Negro Man called Josey, Who ran Away & was out, for the space of three Months or upwards, All which time he daily Comitted thefts and Roberys on his Majesty's Subjects, but having run Away but a small time, before the setting of the County Court, of the Precinct where Your Petitioner dwelt, he could not According to the Course of the law take out a warrt. to the Sherrif, to take the body of the[?] County to Apprehend the Said Slave, and before the Succeeding Court, the Said Slave was shott in the Apprehending of him and killed, After having been run away a longer time than the law prescribes for taking out a Warrant directed to the Sherriff as Aforesaid for Apprehending the Said Slave (which was Occationed by the Courts not Intervening)

    Hee therefore hopes You'l take the same into Consideration & Allow Your Petitioner the value of the Said Slave, which was Adjudged by the County Court of New Hanover, to the Sum of four Hundred Pounds Currency, in as Much As the Said Negroe had been run away, the time Prescribed by the Laws of this Province, giving power in Such Case, to kill Any Slave in Apprehending; And Your Petitioner As in Duty bound, Shall ever pray

Secretary of State Papers
Magistrates Courts

Job Howes

****

North Carolina State Archives
Magistrates and Freeholders Courts, 1715-1793
Secretary of State Papers, Box #311

Ismael, a Slave

Certificate for An Negro
Executed at Onslow County
belonging to Steven Lee

North Carolina }
Onslow County }

    Att a Special Court Summoned and met at New river in the County Afforesd. Agreeable to the Act of the General Assembly relating to Servants & Slaves. An Negro man Calld Ismael belonging to Mr. Stephen Lee, of the sd. County was Capitally Convicted, of **[Torn]** & Felonies by the sd. negro Comitted within the sd. County **[Torn]** Judgment of Death to be Hang'd, the sd. Negro man was Valued by the Justices & ffreeholders that Constitute the sd. Court as Directed by the Law to the sum of Forty Six pounds thirteen Shillg. & four pence **[Torn]** Money, of wch. wee give this Certificate as Witness our hands & Seals this 11th February 1745/6

                      Justices
                    John Starky
                    James Hoyle
                    Abrm. Mitchell
                    Edwd. Ward
                    John Howard

                    Freeholders
                    Anthony Lowrie
                    William Dudley

Secretary of State Papers
Magistrates Courts

Richd. Hair
Francis Burnett

****

North Carolina State Archives
Magistrates and Freeholders Courts, 1715-1793
Secretary of State Papers, Box #311

Jack & Stephen, Slaves

The Examination of Stephen A negro man Slave tryed the 3rd day of December Anno Dom 1748 at a Court held at Bath town, Present John Barrow, John Rieusset, Robert Boyd and James Adams Esqrs.Captn. Seth Pilkington, Captn. Michl. Cotanche, Mr. Daniel Blin & Mr. Richd. Barrow Freeholders.

    The above named Slave named Stephen confesses, that Jack a negro man Slave belonging to Mr. Edward Howcalt on monday night last past being between the 27th and 28th of November last past, he the sd. Jack assisted the said Stephen in braking out of the Goal at Bath town by giving him into the said Goal a piece of Iron about eighteen Inches in length, with which he the said Stephen broke his hand Cufs, and then struck the pad lock off the inward door and the bolt flew back, then he opened the door and came out through a hole which was in the floor of said goal, after which the sd. Jack carried the said Stephen on his back down to Mr. Caita's landing, and over the Creek in a Canoe to Mr. Howcalt's Plantation the next night they came over to Town to get a File, sd. Jack said he woud goe to the Smith Shop to get a file, but came back with out one, there the said Jack said he dare say he could get a file out of that store which was Mr. Simpson's, there the said Jack broke open the Celler door of Mr. Simpson's Stoar with a Chisel and Ax, and there stole three bottles of Rum, then they came from the Celler and broke open the Stoar door with a Chisel and Tomahawk and then entered the sd. Stoar said Jack wrenched open a Chest in said Stoar out of which and said Stoar Stephen took a Watch, Some bisket one worsted Mittan, one Snuff box, and sundry small articles, said Jack carried out of said Stoar one piece of white linen and Sundry small things and carried down and put in his Canoe, from thence they weant from Mr. Rieussets Stoar and tryed to

Secretary of State Papers
Magistrates Courts

brake open the door, then the said Jack weant to the window of said Store and broke a piece of it by trying to wrench it open, at which time he was aprehended by Mr. John Williams, and said Jack made his escape in a Canoe.

Michel Cotanche	J: Barrow
Danl. Blin	R. Boyd
Richard Barrow	James Adams

No. Carolina Beaufort County} At a Court held at the Court house in Bath Town on Saturday the 3rd day of Decr. Anno Dom 1748.

Here Present   }
Esqrs.   }
John Barrow, John Rieusset, Robert Boyd, James Adams

Freeholders}
Captn. Seth Pilkington, Captn. Michl. Cotanche, Mr. Daniel Blin, & Mr. Richd. Barrow

There being committed to the County Goal a negro man Slave named Stephen, the Property (as he Sayeth) of Wm. Sparrel of the Colony of Virginia, which said Slave above mentioned is Committed to the said Goal by Virtue of a Mittimus from Robert Boyd Esqr. one of the Justices assigned to keep the Peace in the said County on Suspicion that he the said Stephen had stole a Mare, Sadle and bridle being the property of Mr. Thomas Lee of Tyrell County in the aforesd. Province Planter, and by another Mittimus he the said Stephen was committed to the Goal aforesd. by John Rieusset Esqr. one of the Majesties assigned to keep the peace in the sd. County of Beaufort for brakeing open a Store belonging to Mr. Charles Simpson of Bath town in the aforesd. County Merchant and feloniously Stealing and carrieing away sundry goods out of the Same Store, viz. one watch, twenty breast mettle buttons, three Jack knives, two snuff boxes, one paper Ink powder, eight bisket, one Stack, one Cravatt, one white worsted mitton, and sundry other small articles. And the said negro man Slave named Stephen being brought in to Court, the Justices And Freeholders within named, did proceed to Try the said Slave, and after examining the said Slave, and hearing the evidence's upon mature Deliberation thereof, the Court think Proper to Respite their Judgement

Secretary of State Papers
Magistrates Courts

untill the thirteenth day of this Instant. Afterwards, to wit, at the Court house in Bath Town on Tuesday the 13th day of this instant December Pursuant to the Foregoing order the Justices and Freeholders herein under written met, viz. John Barrow, John Rieusset, Robert Boyd, and James Adams Esqrs. Justices of the Peace in this County, and Captn. Michl. Cotanche, Mr. Daniel Blin and Mr. Richd. Barrow Freeholders, the sd. Negro Slave named Stephen, within mentioned, was brought into Court by the Sheriff and having nothing to offer to the Court why Sentence of death shoud not pass against him; It was adjudged by the Court that the sd. Stephen shoud return to the County Goal, from whence he came; and from thence tomorrow morning, being the fourteenth day of this present December to be carried to the forenoon to be hanged by the neck, till he be dead, and God Almighty be mercifull to his Soul. The Court do Value the sd. Slave at Thirty five pounds Procl. money.

Michl. Cotanche	J. Barrow
Danl. Blin	R. Boyd
Richard Barrow	James Adams
	John Rieusset

This Claim to be paid to Mr. Ormond for the use of Mr. Sparrell.

****

North Carolina State Archives
Magistrates and Freeholders Courts, 1715-1793
Secretary of State Papers, Box #311

North Carolina Ss:
Bladen County

Will, a Slave

Whereas we the Subscribers Summoned Agreeable to Law on the Tryal of A Negro Man Named Will Belongd. to Georg Corneige Living at Tre[Faded] River Which Sd. Negro Named Will Hath Bene Convicted by Lawfull Evidence of fellowniusly Braking open Houses And Stealing to the Value of Ten Pounds Sterling Money of Great Britian for which

Secretary of State Papers
Magistrates Courts

Centance of Death is Past against him; & Persuant to a Law of this Province We Are Impowred & Directed to Set A Just Value on Sd: Negro: Which We Have Valued to forty Pounds Proclamation Money: as witness Our Hands And Seals This 15th Day of December 1748

        Griffith Jones
        Willm: Bartram
        Saml. Baker
        Tho: O'Neill
        Richard Singeltary
        Willm. Cane
        Thomas Bryan

George Kornegue
Allowed his Claim of
40£ Proclm. Money
April 1749

****

North Carolina State Archives
Magistrates and Freeholders Courts, 1715-1793
Secretary of State Papers, Box #311

North Carolina Ss.
Bladen County

Cain, a Slave

      Whereas we the Subscribers Summond Agreeable to Law on the Tryal of a Negro Caled Cain Belonging to James Baldwin which Sd. Negro is Charged And Lawfully Convicted of feloniously Shooting And Killing John Green Senr: And Persuant to A Law of this Province We Are Impowred And Directed to Set A Just Value on Sd: Negro Which we Value to the Sum of forty Pounds Proclamation Money.
As Witness our Hands and Seals this 29 Day april 1749.

        James Lyon
        Saml. Baker
        William Bartram

Secretary of State Papers
Magistrates Courts

Richard Singeltary
Thomas Bryan
Thos. White
Hugh Blanning

Gentlmn:
Please to Pay the full Contents Above Mentioned Unto Wm: Bartram & His Rect. Shall be a full Discharge from your Most Humbl. Servt. Septr: 23d. 1749.
James Baldwin

Mr. James Baldwin Allowed his Claim for a Negroe Executed.

****

North Carolina State Archives
Magistrates and Freeholders Courts, 1715-1793
Secretary of State Papers, Box #311

North Carolina} The Public to Ralph Miller
Bladen County} Late Shiriff -------- Dr.

for the years 1747 & 1748

To one year & nine months, Sallery -------14
To Executg: a Negroe belonging to George Conegie being Tenn days in my Custody with a Sufficient Guard, five days of the time being in a Public House
To Executg: a Negroe belonging to James Baldwin
To bringing Wm: Turner Gilbert Turner and Edward Turner from Pee Dee to Wilmington There staying 4 days with a Guard of 10: men
There being no efects to be found I hope your Honrs: will Allow me for it.
Ralph Miller

****

North Carolina State Archives
Magistrates and Freeholders Courts, 1715-1793
Secretary of State Papers, Box #311

Secretary of State Papers
Magistrates Courts

Prince, a Slave

Beaufort County Ss. } At a Court convened and held the 16th day of July 1751 at the Court House in Bath Town for the Trial of a Negro named Prince belonging to Mr. Richd. Grise who was Sentenced to Death and Executed accordingly.

Present John Barrow Robt Boyd and Henry Snoad Esqrs.
Justices William Lanier William Willis William Waggenor and Lamuel Cherry freeholders We the afsd freeholders being Sworn to Value the afsd Negro according to the best of our Skill and Judgment Do value the said Negro to fifty pounds money

Test William Ormond Cler Cur

Wm Waggenor Wm Willis R Boyd T Barrow Wm Lanier
Henry Snoad Leml Chery

****

North Carolina State Archives
Magistrates and Freeholders Courts, 1715-1793
Secretary of State Papers, Box #311

Serina, a Slave

North Carolina } Ss.
Chowan County }

At a Special Court called and held at the Court house in Edenton on Friday the Seventeenth of November In the year of our Lord One Thousand Seven hundred & fifty two for the Tryal of a Negroe woman Slave called Serina belonging to Solomon King of Edenton aforesd. pursuant to the Directions of an Act of the General Assembly of the said Province Intitled "An Act concerning Servants and Slaves Which said Negroe was then and there duly convicted of and condemned for felloneously Stealing & carrying away a Chest out of the said Solomon

Secretary of State Papers
Magistrates Courts

King's Store **[Faded]** aforesaid and Stealing out of the sd. Chest the Sum of thirty **[Faded]** Pounds Current Money of the Colony of Virginia being the Property of One Richard Bell

                Present Esquires Justices
                        Thomas Luten
                        Peter Payne
                        John Halsey
              Freeholders & Owners of Slaves
                        William Hoskins
                        William Luten
                        William Arkill
                        Charles Blount

      These may certify that we the said Justices and Freeholders, According to the Directions of the before recited Act do value the said Negroe woman Slave called Serina, at fifty Pounds Proclamation Money And we do hereby further certify that William Mearns acted as Clerk to the said Special Court and that he has not received any Fee or Reward for the SameWitness our Hands & Seals at Edenton the Day & year first above written.

Wm. Arkill	(Seal)	Thos Luten	(Seal)
Wilm. Luten	(Seal)	Peter Payne	(Seal)
William Hoskins	(Seal)	J. Halsey	(Seal)
Charles Blount	(Seal)		

****

North Carolina State Archives
Magistrates and Freeholders Courts, 1715-1793
Secretary of State Papers, Box #311

Cato, a Slave

Sertificate of
Cato tryel
Allowd. 53: 6: 8

Secretary of State Papers
Magistrates Courts

Gentlemen
    Please Pay the Within Contents to Wm. Bartram Esqr.
        Isaac Jones

North Carolina } Ss. Bladen County 27th March 1753
Bladen County   } at a Court held this Day for the

Trial of a Negroe fellow Named Cato the property of Isaac Jones of this County Planter.
    Present John Rutherford, Griffeth Jones & Thomas Turnbull Esqr. Messrs. Thomas Bryan, John Brown, Donald McKiskin and Evan Ellis freeholders & Masters of Slaves.
    The said Negroe fellow Cato was found Guilty of Death for having made an Attempt to Murder Margaret Thomson & Stabing her with a knife to the Great Danger of her Life.
    The said Negroe fellow being Appraised was Valued at fifty three Pounds six Shillings & Eight pence proclamation Money & In order to Enable the said Isaac Jones to Recover the said Money agreeable to the Law of this Province, the Clerk was ordered to make out a Certificate of the Same.

Jno. Jones D: Clerk

Thomas Bryan	John Rutherford
Donald Mc[Faded]	Griffeth Jones
John Brown	Thomas Turnbull
Evan Ellis	

****

North Carolina State Archives
Magistrates and Freeholders Courts, 1715-1793
Secretary of State Papers, Box #311

Tom, a Slave

        February the 10th 1755

Secretary of State Papers
Magistrates Courts

North Carolina   }
New Hanover County   }

      A Court held at the Court house for the Tryal of a Negro Man named Tom belonging to John Duboise Esqr. for breaking open the house of Joshua Toomes and there Stealg rice[?] belong to Da[?] Danbibin

          Cornelius Harnet Esqr.   }
Present John Lyon   } Justices
          Frederick Grag   }

Joshua Toomes   }
John Maultsby   } Freeholders
Joshua Grainger   }
Thos. Cunningham   }

Evidence
Ste[Smudged]   Examnd.
Sam L.   Exam
Cloe   Examnd.
Mariah   Examnd.
Rose   Examnd.

Ordered that the said Negroe Tom belonging to John Duboise Esqr. be Castrated by having both his Stones Cut out.

and in Case he shall die in the opperation or [?] the [?] made we the Justices and freeholders do Value the sd. Negro Tom to be of the Value of Seventy pounds, proclamation Money and in case of any [?] to be allow'd by the publick

Ordered that the Sherrif cause the sd. Negro to be Castrated on or before the 15th of this Instant and that he be in Goal the mean time.
Cornls. Harnett
        his
Thomas T Cunningham   John Lyon
        mark   Fredk. Gragg
Jos Grainger

Secretary of State Papers
Magistrates Courts

Captn. Du Bois Claim for 70.0.0 Allow'd by the Commitee

No Carolina }
New Hanover County }   John Du Bois this Day made
Oath
before me that the Within Mentioned negro man had his full allowance of Corn agreeable to Law
Jno. Du Bois
Sworn before me this 15 Septr 1755
Cornl. Harnett

North Carolina }
New Hanover County } This day came before me Cornelious Harnett Esqr. One of his Majesty's Justices assigned to Keep the Peace for the County aforesd. Isaac Faries Practitioner of Physick and Surgery who being Sworn on the Holy Evangelist of Almighty God, Deposeth & Sayeth

That on the 28th of Febry. last he was calld upon to See a Negro Man Slave named Tom belonging to John DuBois Esqr., who in pursuance of the Sentance of a Court had been Castrated Sometime before, he accordingly went and found him with Convoulsive Motions on the Diaphragm every Minute or two, and Soe cramped backwards, that there was no bending of him forwards, he likewise saw the Wounded parts examined after he was dead, and is of Opinion that the Castration was the cause of his death, He further declares he knew the fellow for several years before and never heard or knew of any disorder he had that could Occasion his death before the Castration, Further Saith not.

Sworn to before me this 15th   Isaac Faries
day of September 1755
Cornl. Harnett J.C.

****

North Carolina State Archives
Magistrates and Freeholders Courts, 1715-1793
Secretary of State Papers, Box #311

Peter, a Slave

Secretary of State Papers
Magistrates Courts

North Carolina }
New Hanover County } These are to Certifie that a Negro Man Named Peter the property of John MacKenzie But have lived Several Years with William MacKenzie In the County & province aforesaid, was aprehended & Tried For Burgulary & Felony & found Guilty & Sentence Passed upon the Said Negro to be hanged which Sentence was Accordingly Executed, & the said Negro was Valued at Eighty pounds proclamation Money as Witness our Hands & Seals who were on the said Tryal 15th March 1757.

Cornl. Harnett (Seal)
Jno. DuBois (Seal)
Fredk. Gregg (Seal)
John Morris (Seal)
James Gregory (Seal)
Danl. Dunbibin (Seal)
   his
Thomas T Cunningham (Seal)
   Mark

John McKinzie was allowed his Claim of 80 for a Negro man Hanged.

****

North Carolina State Archives
Magistrates and Freeholders Courts, 1715-1793
Secretary of State Papers, Box #311

Phoebe & Mary, Slaves

Tryal of two Negro Women
7th Augst. 1757 at Wilmington

At a Court Began & held at Wilmington for the Tryal of Two Negro Women the one Named Phoebe the other named Mary Belonging to Mr Ralph Taylor Phoebe belonging to Mrs McCorkel on Wednesday the 7th Day of Augst. 1757.

Secretary of State Papers
Magistrates Courts

Before Cornelius Harnett }
Jno Lyon } Esqrs.
Armand Derosset }

Danl Dunbibins }
Jno. Morris } Freeholders
Thos Rutledge }
James Campbell }

Evidences their own Certification

Virdict
Judgment Phiba be led with a haulter about her Neck to the place of Execution and there to Receive fifty Lashes well Laid on her bare back.
Mary to be hangd by the Neck at the Place of Public Execution and there hang till she be Dead ye 9th of this Instant Friday Next at 2 O'clock in the afternoon and the said Court Valued the said Slave at Eighty pounds Procl. Money.

This Certifie that the above Negro Wench was Valued by the Court at 80 Procl. Money as above, and Executed at the place of Public Execution agreeable to the above Judgement.
James Moran C Ct.

Cornl. Harnett, John Lyon, Armand De Rosset, Danl. Dunbibin, John Morris, Tho. Routledge, Jas. Campbell

Ralph Taylors Claim of 80.00.0 was Allowed for a Negro wench Hang'd.

****

North Carolina State Archives
Magistrates and Freeholders Courts, 1715-1793
Secretary of State Papers, Box #311

Tom, a Slave

Norfolk County

Secretary of State Papers
Magistrates Courts

Complaint to me one of his Majts Justices of the Peace for the sd County by Robt Tucker that on Saturday the 13th Instant the sd Tuckers house was broke open and Sundry goods stolen from the Robt Tucker to the Value of twenty Shillg Currt money of Virginia.

These are in his Majts Name to Command you to make a Diligent Serch after the said goods & them you having found you are to bring them with the Persons in whosoever Custody you find them with, before me or some other of his Majts Justice of the peace to the sd. County that they may be Delt with according to Law & this shall be your Warrant Given under my hand this 15th of August 1763.
Maxl. Calvert

Norfolk County

I herewith send you the Body of Negro Tom belonging to Capt. Stephen Wright of this County him you are Safly to Keep in your Gole he being Charged with felony & this shall be your Warrant Given under my hand this 15th of August 1763.
Maxl. Calvert

Virginia SS.

Francis Fauquier Esq; His Majesty's Lieutenant Governor, and Commander in Chief of the said Colony and Dominion.

To John Hutchings, William Ivey, Wilson Newton, George Veall, Joshua Corprew, Robert Tucker Junr., William Atchison, Matthew Godfrey, John Tatem, Thomas Veall, Maximilian Calvert, Lemuel Willoughby, and Joseph Hutchings of the County of Norfolk

Gentlemen Greeting

Know Ye, That whereas I have constituted and appointed you Justices of Oyer and Terminer for the Trial of Tom a Negroe Man slave belonging to Captain Stephen Wright for Felony I do therefore by Virtue of the Powers and Authorities to me granted by His Majesty, as Commander in Chief of this Dominion, authorize and appoint, that the Commission being read as usual, any one of you said John Hutchings, William Ivey, Wilson Newton, George Veall, Joshua Corprew, or Robert Tucker having first taken the Oath as appointed by Act of Parliament to be taken, instead of the Oaths of Allegiance and Supremacy the Oath appointed to be taken by an Act of

Secretary of State Papers
Magistrates Courts

Parliament made in the first Year of the Reign of his late Majesty King George the First, Intituled "An Act for the further Security of his Majesty's Person and Government and the Succession of the Crown in the Heirs of the late Princess Sophia, and for extinguishing the Hopes of the pretended Prince of Wales, and his open and Secret Abettors;" as also the Test, together with the Oath for duly executing the Office of a Justice of Oyer and Terminer, which the said William Atchison and Matthew Godfrey or any two in the Commission above named are hereby required and empowered to give and administer to you; you administer to the above Justices, and every of them, in the Commission above named, the above mentioned Oaths and Test, together with the Oath for duly executing the Office of a Justice of Oyer and Terminer, of the performance of which you are to make due Return to the Secretary's Office. Given under my Hand, and the Seal of the Colony, at Williamsburg, the Eighteenth Day of August One Thousand Seven Hundred and Sixty three in the Third of the Reign of our Sovereign Lord King George the Third.
Fran: Fauquier

****

North Carolina State Archives
Magistrates and Freeholders Courts, 1715-1793
Secretary of State Papers, Box #311

Cato, a Slave

North Carolina   } Ss.
Chowan County }

At a Court called at the Court house in Edenton on the fourteenth day of November in the Year of our Lord 1766 for the trial of Negroe Cato the property of the Estate of Henry Bonner deceased for feloniously Ravishing and carnally knowing a certain Elizabeth Fallaw contrary to the Kings peace & so forth.

Present the Worshipfull
Samuel Swift, George Brownrigg & Thomas Bonner Esquires Justices. Messrs. Robert Hardy, George Blair, James Hurst & Samuell Benbury Freeholders & owners of Slaves.

Secretary of State Papers
Magistrates Courts

The Court Qualified according to Law On full proof of the fact with which the said Negroe Cato stands Charged Ordered that he be taken to the place of common Execution by Joseph Blount Esquire or his Deputy Mr Charles Bondfield on Monday the Seventeenth day of this Instant November and Between the hours of twelve & one O'Clock of the same day be fastened to a Stake & there burnt until he be dead and that Elizabeth Bonner administratrix of Henry Bonner deceased be allowed for the said Negroe Cato the Sum of Eighty Pounds Procl. Money the Court in their Judgment thinking that Sum the true value of said Negroe Cato.

Sam: Swift
Thos. Bonner
Geo. Blair
James Hurst

George Brownrigg
Robt. Hardy
Samuel Benbury

Administratrix of Henry Bonners Claim Allowed 80 to the dministratrix.

****

North Carolina State Archives
Magistrates and Freeholders Courts, 1715-1793
Secretary of State Papers, Box #311

Pompey, a Slave

Pompey's Tryal & Condemnation
Octo. 24th 1765

North Carolina Ss.

At a Special Court Holden at the Court House in Hertford County on the Twenty fourth day of October Anno Dom MDCCLXV for the Tryal of One Negroe Man Slave Named Pompey Belonging to Richard Yeates for Attempting the Murther of His said Master, by Seizing Cutting and Wounding him &c.

Present

Secretary of State Papers
Magistrates Courts

John Brown }
Henry Hill } Justices
Math. Brickell }
Robert Hardy }

Isaac Carter }
John Hare } Freeholders
Moses Sumner }
Nicholas Perry }

    We after being Duly Quallified Appointed Benjamin Wynns to Act as Clerk to take and Enter the Proceedings thereof.

    And the Prisoner being Charged With the said Crime And Asked Whether he was Guilty or not Guilty of the Crime wherewith he stood Charged, Confessed that He was Guilty of the Crime as Charged.

    And the Court thereupon after Considering the Matter Maturely and Deliberately was of Opinion that the Prisoner at the Bar was Guilty of Felony in such a Manner as to Deserve Death, And therefore doth Give Judgment that He the said Prisoner should be Hanged by the Neck till he shall be dead on Tuesday the Twenty Ninth day of this Instant Between the Hours of Twelve and three in the afternoon, And that his Head shall be Severed from his Body, And Stuck up on a Stake Below the Cross Road at Mr Ramsays.

    It is also Ordered that the Sheriff see the above Judgment Duly Executed.

    At the same time the Court Vallued the above said Negroe Man Slave to Sixty Pounds Proclamation Money.

John Brown	(LS)	Henry Hill	(LS)
Math. Brickell	(LS)	Robt Hardy	(LS)
Isaac Carter	(LS)	Nicholas Perry	(LS)
John Haren	(LS)	Moses Sumner	(LS)

Copy
Test Benjn. Wynns Cler Cur

Richard Yeates Claim 60 Allowed

****

Secretary of State Papers
Magistrates Courts

North Carolina State Archives
Magistrates and Freeholders Courts, 1715-1793
Secretary of State Papers, Box #311

Dick, a Slave

North Carolina }
Rowan County   }

At a Call Court Held Forthe The Trial of A negro fellow Named Dick The property of John Brevard Esqr. Being A slave.
    Being [Torn] With the Attempt of Murthering his said Master by the wound he gave him and the Attempt of Killing Severell Negroes the property of said Brevard and also his Takeing up Arms Against Divers Subjects who, did Attempt To Take him the sd. Negroe Dick And after hearing the said Severel Charges and Allegations Said against him the Said Dick and after hearing the Proofs from Sufficient Evidence We the Sd. Justices and freeholders Do Order that the Sheriff of this County do Take the said Negroe Dick and him Safely keep untill Wednesday the 30th of This Inst. which day you shall Cause the sd. Slave to be hung by the Neck untill he Is Dead and That you Cause his head to be Choped off and put up at the Forks of the Road that Leads to George Davisons as an Example & This Slave So Condemned and is allowed by said free holders to be Vallued or worth the Sum of Thirty five Pounds Proc. Money

To the Sheriff of Rowan To Execute this p[?]
Richd. Brandon
his R Mark   Jno Brandon
                         Walter [Faded]
Jas Carson   Andrew Allison
                         Robt. Brevard
                         Michael Brown

Negro Dick Warrent
Allowed 35
1 Janry 1768[5?]

Secretary of State Papers
Magistrates Courts

Executed
Wm. Nassery

****

North Carolina State Archives
Magistrates and Freeholders Courts, 1715-1793
Secretary of State Papers, Box #311

Charges attending a Negroe that was Condemned & hanged in
Edgecombe County P/me Thomas Merritt
Jaylor

1765. To witling[?] 31 men two meals and P./ a guarding the prison	3.2
2/d galls Rum	1.1.3
To Witling[?] the negroe that was hanged	15
pd. 2p fetters & 2p hand cuffs & two chains	2.0.0
To putting in Goal & taken out the two Negroes	10
	7.8.11

Errors Exceptd
to Thomas Merritt

Sworn to before me   Jos [?] CC

****

North Carolina State Archives
Magistrates and Freeholders Courts, 1715-1793
Secretary of State Papers, Box #311

Quash, a Slave

North Carolina }
Chowan County } Ss.

Secretary of State Papers
Magistrates Courts

At A Court begun & held at Edenton at the Court House in Edenton on third Day of August in the Year of our Lord One Thousand seven hundred and Sixty Seven for the Tryal of Negroe Quash before

Samuel Swift   }
John Hodgson   }   Esqrs. Justices
Geo. Brownrigg }

Samuel Benbury }
Jeremiah Halsey }   Freeholders and
William Roberts }   Owners of Slaves
John Adams   }

Who took the Oath agreeable to the Act of Assembly in that Case made and Provided; Ordered that Quash a Negroe Fellow of the Property of George Campbell Esqr. in Liverpoole for the Murder of a Negroe Man named London late the property of the Reverend Daniel Earle be carried to the Gaol from where he came & from there to the Common Place of Execution on Tuesday next) between the Hours of Eleven and Twelve and be hanged by the Neck till he be dead it is considered by the Court that the said Quash be of the Value of Seventy Pounds Procl. Money Given under our hands the Day and Year above written.
Test
Fred Blount

        Sam: Swift
        Jno. Hodgson
        George Brownrigg
        Samuel Benbury
        Jer. Halsey
        William Roberts
        John Adams

For Mr Jones
7 Jany
70 Allowed
Execd

****

Secretary of State Papers
Magistrates Courts

North Carolina State Archives
Magistrates and Freeholders Courts, 1715-1793
Secretary of State Papers, Box #311

Quamino, a Slave

At a Court of Magistrates and Freeholders held at the Court house in Wilmington on Monday February 8th 1768 on the Tryal of a Negroe Man named Quamino belonging to the Estate of John DuBois Esqr. Deceas'd, charged with robbing sundry Persons.
Present

Cornelius Harnett	}
John Lyon	}
Frederick Gregg	} Esqrs. Justices
John Burgwine	}
William Campbell	}

John Walker	}
Anthony Ward	} Freeholders & Owners of Slaves
John Campbell	}
William Wilkinson	}

    The Court upon Examination of the Evidences relating to several Robberies committed by Quamino have found him guilty of the several Crimes charg'd against him, and Sentenced him to be hang'd by the Neck until he is dead tomorrow morning between the Hours of ten & twelve O'Clock and his head to be affixed up upon the Point near Wilmington.
    The Court Valued the said Negroe Quamino at eighty Pounds proclamation Money proof having been made, that he had his full allowance of Corn agreeable to Act of Assembly.

Cornls. Harnett Clk

****

North Carolina State Archives
Magistrates and Freeholders Courts, 1715-1793
Secretary of State Papers, Box #311

Secretary of State Papers
Magistrates Courts

Johnny, a Slave

At a Magistrates & Freeholders Court held at the Court house in Wilmington on Monday February 8th 1768 On the Tryal of a Negro Man named Johnny the Property of James Harell Junr. Esqr. Charg'd with Robbing Sundry Persons.

Present
Cornelius Harnet }
John Lyon }
Frederick Gregg } Esquires & Justices
John Burgwin }
William Campbell }

John Walker }
John Campbell } Freeholders & Owners of Slaves
Anthony Ward }
William Wilkinson }

  The Court upon Examination of the Evidence relating to several Robberies committed by Johnny hath found him Guilty of the several Crimes charg'd against him, and Sentenced him to be hang'd by the Neck untill he is dead -- to Morrow Morning between the hours of ten & twelve o'clock, and his head to be affixed upon the New road opposite Wilmington.
  The Court Valued the said Negro Johnny at Eighty pounds proclamation Money, proof having been made that he had his full Allowance of Corn agreeable to Act of Assembly.

Sign'd Corns. Harnett, John Lyon, Frederick Gregg, Wm. Campbell, John Burgwin, William Wilkinson, Anthony Ward, John Walker, John Campbell.

  I hereby Certify that the Aforegoing is a true Copy of the Proceedings on the Tryal of the said Negro Johnny, taken from the Record Lodg'd in the Clerks Office of New Hanover County.

John London C Ct.

Secretary of State Papers
Magistrates Courts

Copy of the Proceedings on the Tryal of Negro Johnny Valued at 80.

Allowed 80

Mr. James Harell Junr. Claim

****

North Carolina State Archives
Magistrates and Freeholders Courts, 1715-1793
Secretary of State Papers, Box #311

Jack, a Slave

North Carolina   }
New Hanover County   } At a Magistrates & Freeholders Court,

held at the Court house in Wilmington on Monday February 8th 1768 On the Trial of a Negro Man Named Jack the property of Doctor John Corbyn for Robbing Sundry Persons.

Present
Cornelius Harnett   }
John Lyon   } Esqrs. Justices
John Burgwin   }

John Walker   }
Anthony Ward   } Freeholders
John Campbell   } Owners of Slaves
Wm. Wilkinson   }

    The Court upon Examination of the Evidences relating to Several Roberies committed by said Jack have found him Guilty of the several Crimes charg'd against him, and Sentenced him to be hang'd by the Neck untill he is dead, tomorrow Morning between the hours of ten & twelve o' Clock. And the Court Valued said Jack at Sixty Pounds Procl. Money, Proof having been made that he had his full Allowance agreeable to Law.

Secretary of State Papers
Magistrates Courts

A true Copy taken from the records Lodged in the Clerks Office of New Hanover County.
John London CC

New Hanover County, Wilmington October the 11th 1769 These may Certify that the within named Negro Jack, was Executed agreeable to law, the ninth day of February 1768 when **[Blotted Out]** was Sheriff of the aforesaid County.
Jas Moran

Doctr. John Corbin allowed his Claim of 60.   1770

****

North Carolina State Archives
Magistrates and Freeholders Courts, 1715-1793
Secretary of State Papers, Box #311

Will, a Slave

At a Magistrates & Freeholders Court held at the Court House in Wilmington on Monday February 28th 1768 on the Tryal of a negro fellow named Will, charg'd with the Murder of his Master Bryant Lee and Mary his Wife.

Present
Frederick Gregg   }
William Purviance   } Esqrs. Justices
John Lyon   }

Anthony Ward   }
William Wilkinson   } Freeholders and Owners
John Campbell   } of Slaves
Samuel Marshall   }

Evidence to prove the Murder
Hudlin Huffham

Secretary of State Papers
Magistrates Courts

The said Negro is found Guilty of the Murder of his Master & Mistress And Ordered that the said Negro fellow Will be hung alive in Gibbets at the Gallows near Wilmington between this & Saturday next the 5th of this Inst. March. The said Negro Valued at Eighty Pounds Procl. Money.

Sign'd John Lyon, Wm. Purviance, Fredk. Gregg. Anth. Ward, William Wilkinson, John Campbell, Saml. Marshall

I hereby Certify that the Aforegoing is a true Copy taken from the Records Lodged in the Clerks Office of New Hanover County & that the Sum of Eighty Pounds Proclamation Money is the Sum of which the said Negro is Valued at Agreeable to Law.

John London   CC

****

North Carolina State Archives
Magistrates and Freeholders Courts, 1715-1793
Secretary of State Papers, Box #311

Ned & Daniel, Slaves

At a Court Called and held at Bute County Court house the 2d. day of May one thousand Seven hundred and sixty Eight For the Tryal of Ned, a slave belonging to John Thornton & Daniel a slave belonging to the Estate of William Williamson Deced: on Suspicion of Felony.

Present
William Johnson   }
Philemon Hawkins   }
James Ransom   }
Jethro Sumner   } Esqrs.
Nathaniel Henderson   }
Thomas Turner   }

John Brown   }
Edward Jones   } Freeholders
William Cheek   }

Secretary of State Papers
Magistrates Courts

Thomas Cook   }

      Ned a Negro Slave belonging to John Thornton and Daniel a Slave belonging to the Estate of William Williamson Deceased being brought before the Court on Suspicion of Poisoning the said William Williamson, and other Misdemeanors, On hearing the Witnesses produced Against them, and all the Circumstances Relating to the said Facts being Considered; The Court are of Opinion that the said Negros Ned & Daniel are guilty of the Crime wherewith they stand Charged, in such a degree as to be Punishable with death, and do Adjudge the said Negro Ned to be of the Value of Seventy five pounds Proc. money and the said Negro Daniel to be of the Value of Eighty pounds Proc. money.

      Ordered the sheriff Execute the Above Judgment on the said Ned & Daniel by hanging them by the Neck till Each of them be dead on Monday the 9th of this Instant between the hours of twelve and three in the afternoon, And accordingly they are Executed.

P Julius Nichols Sheriff

Willm Johnson   John Brown
Philemon Hawkins JP   Thos. Cook
Nathl Henderson   Wm Cheek
James Ransom JP   Edward Jones
Thos. Turner   Jethro Sumner

John Thornton & Martha Williamson of Bute allowed 155
19th Decr. 1770

Williamson   }
    &   } Certif.
Thornton   }

****

North Carolina State Archives
Magistrates and Freeholders Courts, 1715-1793
Secretary of State Papers, Box #311

Secretary of State Papers
Magistrates Courts

Cudjo, a Slave

At an Inferior Court of Pleas & Quarter Sessions held for the County of New Hanover at the Court House in Wilmington on the first Tuesday in October 1768.

Present
The Worshipful
Cornelius Harnett	} Esqrs.	his
Frederick Jones	}	Majesty's
William Purviance	}	Justices
John Burgwin	}	

    The Court upon the Application of William Campbell Esqr. for the Valuing a Negro fellow named Cudjo belonging to the said William, who had been run away, and thereupon been Outlawed Agreeable to Law, and upon being taken, the said Negro Cudjo Jumped off the Bridge made over North East river of Cape Fear, into said River and was drowned, And upon Examination of William Jones upon Oath, respecting the Value of the said Negro, They are of Opinion that the said Negro man be Valued at Eighty Pounds Proclamation Money. And Ordered that a Certificate be prepared accordingly so Say before the General Assembly for their final Allowance of the said Sum.

I hereby Certify that the Aforegoing is a true Copy taken from the Court Minutes Lodg'd in the Clerks Office of New Hanover County.

John London C.Ct.

Copy of the Order of Court for the Valuing of Mr. Campbells Negro Man Cudjo.

Allowed 80

****

North Carolina State Archives
Magistrates and Freeholders Courts, 1715-1793
Secretary of State Papers, Box #311

Secretary of State Papers
Magistrates Courts

[Editor's note: This is not Magistrates Record. It is a Court order to bind out free negroes.]

At a Superior Court of Justice began and held at New Bern for the District of New Bern for the Term of May in the Year of our Lord One Thousand Seven Hundred and Sixty Nine.

Present
The Honble. Martin Howard Esqr. Chief Justice
The Honble. Maurice Moore Esqr. Associate Justice

The King at ye suggestion of Amye Moore & Others free negroes
vs
Justices Beaufort

Certiriori to remove ye proceedings & Order of ye Justices of ye Inferior Court of Beaufort Co. for ye Binding out the free Negroes as sd. Order Mentd. & the sd. Proceedings & Order being in Obedience to ye sd. Writ of Certiorior before ye Chief Justices Judgment of this Court Certified & being inspected & maturely condidered ye sd Proceedings & Order are Ordered and Adjudged being illegal [Editor's Note: The rest of this document is missing].

****

North Carolina State Archives
Magistrates and Freeholders Courts, 1715-1793
Secretary of State Papers, Box #311

Toney, a Slave

The Death Warrant of Toney, belonging to Mr Fras. Clayton
June 1769

At a Magistrates & Freeholders Court held at the Court House in Wilmington on Thursday the 8th Day of June 1769.

Secretary of State Papers
Magistrates Courts

Present
Frederick Gregg   }
George Parker   } Esquires Justices
John Ancrum   }

Anthony Ward   }
John Quince   } Freeholders
Richard Bradby   }
William Evans   }

On the Tryal of a Negroe Man Slave Named Toney, the Property of Francis Clayton, being Charg'd of Robing His Master; The Prisoner confess'd the Robery which **[Faded]** of the second Offence, Ordered that he be carrid to the usual place of Execution Tomorrow between the Hours of Ten and Twelve O'Clock in the Forenoon, then and there to be hang'd by the Neck untill He shall be Dead.
Order'd that the Sheriff do Execution accordingly.

By Order of Court
JS Benton   Clerk

****

North Carolina State Archives
Magistrates and Freeholders Courts, 1715-1793
Secretary of State Papers, Box #311

Will, a Slave

The Deposition of Doctr. Thos. Hall
1771

Eliz. Blanings Claim Alld. 80

Doctor Thomas Hall of full Age, maketh Oath on the holy evangelist of Almighty God, that on or about the 30th of July 1769, this deponant was informed by several of his own Negroe Slaves, that a certain Negroe Will, the property of Mrs: Elizabeth Blaning, had declared that he would Poison

Secretary of State Papers
Magistrates Courts

Mrs. Lucy Hall, the Wife of the Deponent: Whereupon this Deponent, some few days afterwards, applyed to Ralph Miller a Magistrate of Bladen County, who thereupon issued his Warrant for apprehending the said Negroe Will, and directed the same to John Maultsby a Constable in the County aforesaid, who in pursuance thereof, on the 7th: day of August in the Year aforesaid, seized and apprehended the said Negroe Will; that being so seized, the said Negroe Will, within two hours thereafter, died in custody of the Constable aforesaid, previously confessing to this Deponent and the said Constable, that he did intend to have given a Dose of something to the said Mrs: Hall to make [Torn] easy. And this Deponent further sayeth that [Torn] the said Negroe Will / apprehending, that the crime with which he stood charged by the testimony of the several Negroe Slaves above mentioned together with his own confession would forfeit his life / did himself take the same Dose of Poison which he had intended to administer to Mrs: Hall, & that he died thereof. This Deponent further sayeth, that he thinks in his conscience, that the said Negroe Will was worth, at the time of his Death, 150 Proclamation Money. And further this Deponent sayeth not.

Sworn to before me this   Thos. Hall
21st day of August 1769

M Moore

****

North Carolina State Archives
Magistrates and Freeholders Courts, 1715-1793
Secretary of State Papers, Box #311

Peter & Essex, Slaves

Pasquotank Court house 10th Novr 1769

These may Certify that we the subscribing justices of the peace for the county and Freeholders, owners of slaves at a court held here agreeably to act of Assembly for the trial of two slaves viz Peter and Essex, the property of Richard Brownrigg Esqr. of Chowan county - found then

Secretary of State Papers
Magistrates Courts

guilty of certain crimes meriting capital punishment and therefore condemned them to be hanged and at the request of the said Richard Brownrigg agreeably to the act of Assembly proceeded to Value the said Slaves, and we do certify that the said Slaves Peter & Essex are each of them of the value of eighty pounds proclamation money that is the two are worth one hundred and sixty pounds   in witness whereof we have subscribed our hands & seals.

Joseph Reding	Wm Boyd	(Seal)
Trimagain Reding	Thos Macknight	(Seal)
Benja. Peddwick	Matthias Ellegood	(Seal)
William Reed	Isaac Gifford	(Seal)
	Abram Symond	(Seal)
	John Sawyer	(Seal)

Pasquotank County Ss.
   Certified that the above named Negro Slaves Peter & Essex the property of Richard Brownrigg Esqr. capitally convicted as above mentioned were by me Executed by hanging by the Neck till they were dead the 12th November 1769.
Isaac Gregory

Richd. Brownrigg Esqr.
Claim of 160
alld. 17th Decr. 1770

****

North Carolina State Archives
Magistrates and Freeholders Courts, 1715-1793
Secretary of State Papers, Box #311

Cuff, a Slave

N. Carolina	}
Onslow County	}
Court House	}
Novr. 23 1769	}

Secretary of State Papers
Magistrates Courts

Certificate of a Tryal of a Negro Slave named Cuff Belonging to the Estate of Benjamin Ward deceas'd taken on Suspicion of poisoning his Late Master. The Sheriff Returnd that he had Summoned the Justices & Freeholders to Sitt on Tryal.

The Court after Strictly Examining the Said Evidences & Maturely Considering the Facts are of Oppinion that the said Negro Cuff is Guilty - and on said Virdict award Execution. Orderd That the said Negro Cuff Return to Prison and from thence to the place of Execution There to be hangd by the Neck on Saturday next between the hours of 2 & 3 Clocke untill he is dead -- Orderd the Sheriff put said Sentence into Execution accordingly - And the said Court Certifies That the Value said Negro at Sixty Pounds procl.

James Howard	(Seal)
Thos. Johnston	(Seal) J.P.
Benajah Dotey	(Seal)
Jas. Kibble	(Seal)
Nat. Hancocke	(Seal)
Geo. Brack	(Seal)
John Pound	(Seal)
Moses Cox Junr.	(Seal)

> The Publick of N. Carolina
> To Mary Ward Dr.
> Novr. 1769 for her Negro
> Man Cuff hangd
> Valued at 60
>
> allowed 17th Decr. 1770
>
> said Negro was hangd
> Certified by Wm. Cray CC

****

North Carolina State Archives
Magistrates and Freeholders Courts, 1715-1793

Secretary of State Papers
Magistrates Courts

Secretary of State Papers, Box #311

Casar, a Slave

North Carolina } Ss.
Chowan County }

At a Court Called at the Court house in Edenton on the twenty third day of March in the Year of our Lord one thousand seven hundred and Seventy for the trial of Casar a Negroe fellow the property of Mr. Mills Reddick of the Colony of Virginia for the Murder of Mr. James Bond late of Chowan County deceased.

Present the Worshipfull
John Benbury	} Esquires Justices
Joseph Hewes	} of Chowan
George Blair	} Inferior Court
Luke Taylor	} Freeholders
John Smith	} owners of
Henderson Standing	} Slaves
Gilbert Leigh	}

The Court Met and Qualified according to Law. It was then and there ordered the fact being fully proved that Casar the Prisoner at the Bar be taken from hence to be carried to the Goal of this County and there remain untill to morrow the twenty fourth day of this instant March and between the hours of twelve O'Clock and four O'Clock in the afternoon of the same day be taken by the Sheriff of the County of Chowan from the Goal of the County aforesaid to the Place of Common Execution and there to be hanged by the Neck untill he the said Casar be dead and it is further considered by the Court that Mr. Mills Reddick the owner of the said Casar be allowed the Sum of Eighty Pounds proclamation Money.

Given under our hands this 23d day of March Anno Dom 1770.

John Benbury	Joseph Hewes
Geo Blair	Luke Taylor
John Smith	Hend: Standing

Secretary of State Papers
Magistrates Courts

Gilbert Leigh

Chowan County} Ss.
    Certified that the above named Negro Fellow called Casar the property of Mr Mills Riddick capitally convicted as above mentioned was by me executed the 24th day of March 1770
Thos: Benbury Sheriff

Trial Negroe Casar
Mills Reddick Claim
Alld. 80

****

North Carolina State Archives
Magistrates and Freeholders Courts, 1715-1793
Secretary of State Papers, Box #311

George, a Slave

No Carolina   }
Duplin County } Ss.

At a Special Court begun & held for the County of Duplin, on the First Day of May, and in the Year of our Lord One Thousand Seven Hundred and Seventy for the Tryal of a Negroe fellow named George, The Property of James Moore Who Stands accused of Committing a Rape on the Body of Jane Rynchy.

Present The Honble. John Sampson}
Thomas Routledge   } Justices
Richd. Clinton   }
James Kenan   }

Gabriel Holmes   }
Archibald Bell   } Freeholders
Burwell Lanier   }
Owen Kenan   }

Secretary of State Papers
Magistrates Courts

The Justices and Freeholders aforesaid being Sworn after having Duly Examined the Several Evidences on their Oaths, do say that the said Negroe George the Prisoner at the Barr, is Guilty of the Rape of which he Stands Charged and have valued the said Slave to Eighty Pounds Proclamation Money **[Torn]** do Order that the said Prisoner be taken from the Barr to the Place of Execution, and there hang by the Neck untill he be dead, and then his head to be Severed from his Body and Stuck up at the Forks of the Road.

John Sampson }
Thos Routledge } Justices
Richd. Clinton }
James Kenan }

Gabriel Holmes }
Archd. Bell } Freeholders
Burwell Lanier }
Owen Kenan }

Certified by Jas. Sampson   CC

Clerks fees for Holding the Court --

James Moore Claim
Allowed
14th Decr. 1770

****

North Carolina State Archives
Magistrates and Freeholders Courts, 1715-1793
Secretary of State Papers, Box #311

Annis, Phillis & Lucy, Slaves

North Carolina }
Beaufort County } Ss.

Secretary of State Papers
Magistrates Courts

This Certifies that at a Special Court Met on the 21st Day of July 1770.

Present, his Majestys Justices and Freeholders, John Barrow, Thomas Respess[?], Thomas Bonner, & William Brown, Justices -- Aaron Windley, William Tripp, John Woodard & Handcock Custis Freeholders Masters of Slaves.

Annis a Negro Wench the Property of Henry Ormond Esqr. Decd. being Examined Relative to the Murder of her said Master Henry Ormond and by her Confession and the Evidence produced Agt. her is found to be Guilty And therefore the said Annis, is Vallued by the Court to be Worth Seventy Five pounds Proc. Money, And Phillis to be Worth Twenty pounds like Money. And Lucy the property of the Estate of Wyrcott Ormond Esqr. Decd. to be Worth Sixty Five pounds Proc. Money, who are found Guilty of the Murder of the said Henry Ormond Given Under our Hands & Seals this 21st Day of July Anno Dom 1770.

Hancock Custis	(Seal)	T Barrow	(Seal)
Aaron Windley	(Seal)	Thos Respess	(Seal)
John Woods	(Seal)	Tho Bonner	(Seal)
Willm. Trippe	(Seal)	Wm. Brown	(Seal)

****

North Carolina State Archives
Magistrates and Freeholders Courts, 1715-1793
Secretary of State Papers, Box #311

Cuff, a Slave

North Carolina }
Beaufort County } Ss.

At a Special Court Called on the Twenty Fifth Day of July in the Tenth Year of his Majestys Reign Ano Dom: 1770

Present
Thomas Bonner } Esqrs.

Secretary of State Papers
Magistrates Courts

Alexr. Stewart }
Willm. Brown   } Justices

Aaron Windley } Freeholders
Henry Lockey   } Masters of
John Warwick   } Slaves
John Newman   }

These are to Certifie that a Negro Man Slave Called Cuff late the Property of Henry Ormond Esqr. Decd. was Apprehended and Brought before the Court, to be Tryed for Aiding and Assisting, in the Murder of his said Master, And by his Own Confession, And the Witness Produced agt. him, is by the Court found Guilty of the Murder, And is Condemned to Die, And Executed, And the Court Vallued him to be Worth Eighty Pounds Proclamation Money, Given Under our Hands & Seals this 25th Day of July Anno Domini, 1770.

Aaron Windley (Seal)   Thos Bonner   (Seal)
Hen: Lockey   (Seal)   Alexr: Stewart   (Seal)
John Warwick   (Seal)   Wm. Brown   (Seal)
John Newman   (Seal)

Certificate of Negro Cuff's
Valuation
80.0.0 procl.

****

North Carolina State Archives
Magistrates and Freeholders Courts, 1715-1793
Secretary of State Papers, Box #311

Seip, a Slave

At a Court held at the Court House in New Bern on Monday the 4th February 1771. For the Trial of Seip a Negroe Slave the property of James Coor being Charged by Mary Worsley of Burglary in Breaking into the House of the said Mary on the night of the 29th Ulto. and threatening

Secretary of State Papers
Magistrates Courts

the life of the said Mary and other Wrongs then and there Feloniously Committed.

Present
Richard Blackledge   }
Richard Cogdell   } Esquires
Frederick Becton   } Justices

Timothy Clear   }
Samuel Frazier   } Gentlemen Freeholders
Levi Dawson   } and Owners of
William Good   } Slaves

The Prisoner being Charged in Court pleaded not Guilty, thereupon the said Mary [Torn] being duly Sworn [Torn] to the Several Charges [Torn] the said Seip which upon the further [Torn]ny of Joseph Ashbury the Facts Alledged against the said Seip being fully proved. The Court was Unanimously of Opinion that the said Negro Seip is Guilty. Ordered that the Sheriff of Craven County Cause the said Slave Seip to be Hanged by the Neck untill he be Dead on Fryday next. And the Court further Certify that the Value of the said Slave is Eighty Pounds Proclamation Money.

Given under our Hands and Seals

Richd. Blackledge   (Seal)
Richd. Cogdell   (Seal)
Fredk. Becton   (Seal)
Timo. Clear   (Seal)
Sam Frazier   (Seal)
Wm. Good   (Seal)
Levi Dawson   (Seal)

****

North Carolina State Archives
Magistrates and Freeholders Courts, 1715-1793
Secretary of State Papers, Box #311

Secretary of State Papers
Magistrates Courts

[Editor's Note: This is not a Magistrates Court Record. It is a penalty levied upon one Stephen Smith for failing to appear at a Muster.]

North Carolina }
Hyde County } Ss.

    Whereas it apears to that Stephen Smith has neglected to appear at my Muster acording to law [?] Where by he has incurred the penalty prescribed by Law

These are therefore to order and we require you to [?] on the goods and Chatles of the said Stephen Smith on so much thereof as shall be Sufficient to satesfy the sum of five Shillings procl. money and for your so doing this shall be your Warrent given under my Hand and   (Seal)
thirsday July 1773   Tho: gaylord
to Benjamin gaylord   Sargent

Executed and returnd
by me Benj gaylord

****

North Carolina State Archives
Magistrates and Freeholders Courts, 1715-1793
Secretary of State Papers, Box #311

North Carolina }
Craven County }

At an Inferior Court of Pleas & Quarter Sessions begun & held at the Court House in the County aforesaid on the second Tuesday of September AD 1775 Before his Majesty's Justices for said County.

May it please your Worships

    Abner Nash of the County aforesaid Gentleman gives your Worships to understand and be informed that a certain Nathaniel Guinn of the County aforesaid Labourer hath been guilty of trading with and

Secretary of State Papers
Magistrates Courts

buying a certain Quantity of Indigo from a Negro Man Slave called Will the Property of your Informant, to the Value of ten pounds Proc. Money Contrary to Law. Wherefore your Complainant humbly prays that the legal Process may Issue & the said Guinn be compelled to answer this Information. And as in Duty bound your Informant shall ever pray.

Jno. Cooke Atty. Pr Guinn

****

North Carolina State Archives
Magistrates and Freeholders Courts, 1715-1793
Secretary of State Papers, Box #311

Gibby, a Slave

State of N. Carolina }
Brunswick County }
      This is to Certifie that at a Court Called in Brunswick on the 18th day of March 1777, for the trial of five Negroe Men who were concerned in the Murder of Mr Henry Williams. That Gibby a Negroe man slave the Property of Mr Samuell Dwight was found Guilty and Sentenced to be Hanged till he was dead dead dead and his head cut off and Stuck upon a pole this side of Lockwoods folly Bridge,
That the said Slave was Valued at Eighty pounds proc Money.
Certified by Order of Court   Will Etord[?]
No. 32 Mr Samuel Dwight Claim for a Negroe Gibbey 80

Isaac, a Slave

State of N. Carolina }
Brunswick County }
      This is to Certifie that at a Court Called in Brunswick County the 18th day of March 1777, for the trial of five Negroe Men who were concerned in the Murder of Mr Henry Williams. That Isaac a Negroe Man Slave the property of Mrs Dupree was found Guilty and Sentenced to be burnt alive, That the said Slave was Valued at Eighty pounds proc Money.

Secretary of State Papers
Magistrates Courts

Certified by Order of Court   Will Etord[?]
No. 31 Mrs. Duprees Claim for Negroe Isaac [Faded]

Toney, a Slave

State of N Carolina   }
Brunswick County   }
    This is to Certifie that at a Court Called in Brunswick County on the 18th day of March 1777 for the trial of five Negroe Men who were concerned in the Murder of Mr Henry Williams, That Toney a Negroe lad Slave the property of Mr Peter Allston was found Guilty and Sentenced to be burnt alive, That the said Slave was Valued at Eighty pounds proc Money.
Certified by Order of Court   Will Etord[?]
No. 29 Peter Alston Claim for Negroe Toney [Faded]

****

North Carolina State Archives
Magistrates and Freeholders Courts, 1715-1793
Secretary of State Papers, Box #311

Jim, a Slave

At a Justices & Freeholders Court held at Wilmington on Saturday the 19th July 1777 on the Tryal of Jim a Negroe Slave the Property of Benjamin Clark of Bladen County Charged with Stealing &c.

Present
William Purviance }	
Thomas Bloodworth }	Justices
Jonathan Dunbiben }	
Erasmus Hanson }	
Thos. Brown }	Jurors, &
Thos. Blake }	Owners of
Geo. McCulloch }	Slaves

Secretary of State Papers
Magistrates Courts

Evidences Sworn
Alexr. Rouse
Geo. St. George
Geo. Brown

Rose, A Negroe Wench, belonging to Geo. McCulloch; Examined

After the Examination of the above Evidences Said Negroe Fellow Jim, was found Guilty of having Stealg. Killing Cattle, & Hoggs & threatening the Lives of Several persons & breakg. open Houses.

Following Sentence was pass'd Upon Said Jim, by Said Court; that he be kept in Safe Custody untill Monday the 21st Inst. & then Conveyed to the place of Execution at 11 O'Clk & there to be hanged by the Neck untill he be dead. The Said Negroe Jim was Vallued by the above Justices & Jurors at the Sum of Eighty pounds Current Money of the State of North Carolina.

Extract from the Minutes
John DuBois   Pro Clk

****

North Carolina State Archives
Magistrates and Freeholders Courts, 1715-1793
Secretary of State Papers, Box #311

Titus, a Slave

State of North Carolina }
Onslow County   }

August the 20th 1777, James Howard Esqr. Committed a certain Negroe Slave named Titus, belonging to John Evans, for committing a rape on Julin Rogers.

Thomas Johnston Esqr. Sheriff, returned that he had Summon'd William Cray, James Howard, Benajah Doty, and John Brin**[Torn]** Esquires, Obed Williams, Stephen Williams, Robert Nixon, Arthur Averitt, Henchee

Secretary of State Papers
Magistrates Courts

Warren, George Mitchell, and Matthew Green, and Holston Roberts, Freeholders, which composed the said Court.

The Court having heard the Evidence and maturely considering the Facts, are Unanimously of Opinion that the said Negro Titus, is Guilty, as he Stands Charged.

And on said Verdict, [Torn] Cha[Torn] pronounced Sentenced & order Execution (to wit) Ordered that the Sheriff take the said Negro Slave Titus, from hence and secure him till the day the 28th Inst. then to be Carried to the place of Execution, & there to be Hanged by the Neck till he is Dead, then his Body to be Burnt.

Ordered the Sheriff [Faded] said [Faded] into Execution, said Court Valued said Negroe Titus to Two Hundred pounds.

Witness Our Hands and Seals August 25th 1777

Willm. Cray	(Seal)	
Jas. Howard	(Seal)	
Benajah Dotey	(Seal)	Justices
John Brinion	(Seal)	
Steph. Williams	(Seal)	
Robt. Nixon	(Seal)	
Obed Williams	(Seal)	
Arthur Averett	(Seal)	Freeholders
Geo. Mitchell	(Seal)	
Matthew Green	(Seal)	his M mark
Henchee Warran	(Seal)	his H mark
Holston Roberts	(Seal)	

Onslow these may certifie That I did Execute the Above Negro Titus   Thos. Johnston Sheriff

true Copy Test Wm. Cray CC

Certificate from Onslow

Secretary of State Papers
Magistrates Courts

Wm. Cray junr. CC

****

North Carolina State Archives
Magistrates and Freeholders Courts, 1715-1793
Secretary of State Papers, Box #311

Esther, a Slave

Tryal & Judgment of Negroe
Woman Esther
James Blount
Jn. H. Comr. 22 Novr. 1786

At a Court held at the Court House in Edenton Pursuant to the several Acts of Assembly made for the Tryal of Slaves, the XVth Day of april in the year of our Lord one thousand Seven hundred & Seventy Nine, for the Tryal of Negro Esther the property of James Blount Esqr. Charged with having given to her Mistress the Wife of the said James Blount a Quantity of Verdigreace in some Tea with Intent to Poison her.

Present
Joseph Hewes	}
William Boyd	} Esqrs. Justices
John Horniblow	}
William Bennett	} Esqrs. Justices
Joseph Underhill	}
John Beasley	}
John Green	} Freeholders & Owners
Jeremiah Haughton	} of Slaves
Joseph Wilkins	}

The Court Qualified agreeable to Law & proceeded to the Tryal of Negro Esther and having the Evidences Against her do find the said Negro Wench Esther Guilty of the Crime she stands Charged with. And that the said Negro Wench be Hanged by the Neck until she be dead and that this Sentence be carried into Execution by the Sheriff of Chowan County on

Secretary of State Papers
Magistrates Courts

Monday the Nineteenth of this Instant April, between the Hours of ten & two O'clock of the said day at the Common Place of Execution Further Ordered that the Sheriff of Chowan County keep the said Negro Wench Esther in safe Custody until the day of Execution.

The Court took into Consideration the Valuation of the said Negro Wench Esther and as the Law now stands the Court are of Oppinion they cannot Value the said Wench to more than Eighty Pounds, altho' they think as Slaves now sell their Worth Eight hundred Pounds. Joseph Hewes, William Boyd, John Horniblow, William Bennett, John Green, Joseph Underhill, John Beasly, Jeremiah Haughton, Joseph Wilkins.

A true Copy Examined by [?]
James Blount Clk of Chowan County Court
These may Certify that the within named Negro Esther was executed by order of the within named Court By Evan Skinner then Sheriff Mr. Blount was allowed the Sum of Forty Pounds in Consequence of the within Sentence & Execution &c. at an Assembly held at Fayetteville Decr. 1786   J. Hunt CHC

****

North Carolina State Archives
Magistrates and Freeholders Courts, 1715-1793
Secretary of State Papers, Box #311

Simon, a Slave

Montgomery County July 19th 1779
At a Called Court held for the Tryal of Simon a negro Slave Supposed to belong to Benj. Hix of the State of South Carolina for Felony.
Present

Benj. Baird	}	
Wm. Mask	}	Justices
Alexr. Baird	}	
John Jennings	}	Gentlemen
Robert Siviret	}	Free holders

Secretary of State Papers
Magistrates Courts

Thomas Jennings } and owners
John Smith   } of Slaves

The Prisoner being broat to the Bar and being permited to speak for him self thereupon the Prisoner Pleads not Guilty.

Severall Witnesses Being Sworn and Examined on the facts it is the Opinion of the Court that he is Guilty, & therefore Sentence him to Death was pronounc'd against him.

The Members of the said Court has Valued the sd. Slave at one Thousand Pounds and Ordered his Execution to be this Day Between the hours of three and five and thereupon the Court adjournd.

one Thousand Pounds   }
N: Carrolina Currency }
Benj. Baird   (Seal)
Wm. Mask   (Seal)
Alexr. Baird   (Seal)
Jno. Jenings   (Seal)
Robert Sivreat   (Seal)
Thos. Jenings   (Seal)
John Smith   (Seal)

****

North Carolina State Archives
Magistrates and Freeholders Courts, 1715-1793
Secretary of State Papers, Box #311

Prince, a Slave

We the Subscribers Being A Court that Tried & Condemned A Negroe man the Property of Robert Jarmain Agreeable to An Act of Assembly of this State Do Value the said Negroe Prince to be Worth Seventy two thousand Pounds Currency **[Note: This value has to be a mistake]** of the State of North Carolina Witness Our Hands & Seals this Twenty fifth Day of Jany. 1783.

Robert Grimes   Eml. Simmons   (Seal)

Secretary of State Papers
Magistrates Courts

Lemuel Hatch J: A.B. Simmons   (Seal)
Ezekl: Clifton   Edmund Hatch   (Seal)
Joseph Reasonover   Esquires

State of North Carolina
Jones County
Robert Germain alld. for the within named Negro 36,000 May 1783

****

North Carolina State Archives
Magistrates and Freeholders Courts, 1715-1793
Secretary of State Papers, Box #311

Arthur, a Slave

> Tryall Negroe
> Slave the Property
> of John Jones Esqr.
> Allowed œ50
> Transcript

North Carolina   }
Halifax County Ss. }

Att a Special Court Call'd and Convened in Halifax Town on the Second day of July Anno Dom 1785 for the Tryall of a Negroe Man Slave Named Arthur, the Property of John Jones Esquire, for Sundry Felonies.

The Worshipfull Present
Nicholas Long   }
Montfort Elbeck   } Esquires Justices
Gao[?] Davis   }

Bridgiman Joyner   }
Henry Joyner   } Free holders and Owners
Hancle[?] Gee   } of Slaves
John B. Ash   }

145

Secretary of State Papers
Magistrates Courts

Who Were duly Qualified, and proceeded to the Tryall of said Slave Arthur;
Whereupon the Court having heard and fully Considered all the Evidences adjudg'd both for and against the Said Arthur the prisoner, do adjudge that he is guilty of the Several crimes, Charged to him, and that he be punished with death and that the Sheriff do execution thereof Friday the 8th July 1785 and also do Value the said Slave Arthur, to the Sum of One Hundred pounds.

Wm. Wooten CCt.

In House of Com 22 Novr. 1785. On motion of Mr. Montfort seconded by Mr. Cabarrus referred to Comee of Claims By Order   J. Hunt Clk.
In Senate Nov. 22   1785 referred as by the House of Commons By order J. Haywood Clk. M. Montfort & M. Cabarrus

****

North Carolina State Archives
Magistrates and Freeholders Courts, 1715-1793
Secretary of State Papers, Box #311

Toney, a Slave

Record of a Court called in Bladen County for the Tryal of a negroe Man Slave named Toney late belonging to the Estate of George Gibbs decd.

The State of North Carolina   }
Bladen County   }
We the Subscribers being Duly Summond; as a Court to Try A Certain Negroe Fellow Toney the Property of the Estate of George Gibbs Esqr. Deceast   Accur'd[?] And Found guilty of the Wilfull Murdering and Burning of A Certain James Thrift; of Sd. County; And After hearing Evidences; And strict inquiry Made Sentance the said Negroe Toney to be Tyed; or Chaind to a Stake there to be Burnt to Death;
And Agreeable to an Act of Assembly in Such Caise Made And Provided We the sd. Court Doth Value the sd. Negroe Toney to the Sum of one

Secretary of State Papers
Magistrates Courts

hundred and Fifty Pounds Given Under Our hand this 2 of August 1785 at Elizabeth Town.

Wm. McRee   JP
Wm. Kirkpatrick   JP
Jno. Brown   JP

JW Bradley F. Holders
Jas. Moorhead
Wm. Oliphant
B [?]

In Senate Nov. 29th 1785
read and referred to the Coms. of Claims By Order J. Haywood   Clk

In House 29 Novr. 1785
referred as by the Senate By Order J. Hunt Clk
75 allowed in money

****

North Carolina State Archives
Magistrates and Freeholders Courts, 1715-1793
Secretary of State Papers, Box #311

Cato, a Slave

Halifax County Ss.

At a Special Court Called & Convened in Halifax Town on Wednesday the 17th day of August Anno Domini 1785 for the Tryall of a Negro Man Slave the Property of William Powell Senr. of Edgcomb County Named Cato, for Murdering a Certain John Miller and a Certain Sarah Gold, on Friday Night the 12th Instant August.

Present the Worshipfull,
Nicholas Long   }
Thomas Tabb   } Esquires

Secretary of State Papers
Magistrates Courts

Jeremiah Helms }

Robert Ward }
Ambrose Harper } Free holders & Owners
Howell Gee } of Slaves
Lovatt Burgess }

Who were qualified agreeable to law by taking the following Oath, to Wit, you and each of you Shall Swear that you will well & Truly Try Negro Cato, the Property of William Powell of Edgecomb County for on a Charge of Murdering a Certain John Miller & a Certain Sarah Gold, and a True Judgmt. give According to your Evidence So help you God

Whereupon the Court having heard the Evidence, Together with all Pregnant Circumstances, attending sd. Cause & having Maturely Considered The Same and Also having Valued the Sd. Negro to One Hundred and Eighteen Pounds Eleven Shillings & five pence Current Money of this State, do Order & Adjudge that the said Cato, be Carried from hence to the Common Prison, & from Thence to the Place of Execution there to be Hanged by the Neck untill Dead & That his head be Severed from his body and Stuck on a Pole at The fork of the Road leading from Enfield Old Court house to fishing Creek Meeting house, and that his body be Consumed by fire, at the Place of Execution, and it is further Order'd, that the Sheriff of Halifax do Execution of the Above Execution of the Above Judgement On Monday the 22d. day of August in the present Year between the hour of Eleven in the fore noon & One in the Afternoon

       Signed by Order
        A Copy
        Test.
       Wm. Wooten Clk.

Wm. Powell Senr.
59.5.7
Money Allowed

****

North Carolina State Archives

Secretary of State Papers
Magistrates Courts

Magistrates and Freeholders Courts, 1715-1793
Secretary of State Papers, Box #311

State of North Carolina Montgomery County

We the Subscribers being part of Call'd Court in the sd. County on July the 19th 1779 for to try a Sertain Negroe fellow Simon Which We Beleav'd to be the property of Capt. Benjamin Hix of South Carolina, And at that time the Court Valued the sd. Slave in Dollar Bills of Creadit; But at the Request of Capt. Hix we the Subscribers doe Recommend that the said Slave to be worth one hundred and twenty pounds Specie.

Sertified From under our hands and Seals this 24th of August 1785.

Wm. Mast	(Seal)
Alexr. Baird	(Seal)
Jno. Jenings	(Seal)
Thos. Jenings	(JP)

****

North Carolina State Archives
Magistrates and Freeholders Courts, 1715-1793
Secretary of State Papers, Box #311

Hercules & Cesar, Slaves

State of North Carolina }
Chowan County }

At A Called Court at the Court House in **[Torn]** the Twenty Third day of February 1780, **[Torn]** Negroe Man Slave Namely Hercules **[Torn]** Lois Worley & Cesar the Property of **[Torn]** For Felony.

Present
Thomas Benbury }
Thomas Barker }
William Bennett }

149

Secretary of State Papers
Magistrates Courts

Robert Patterson }
Gilbert Leigh }
Geo. Gray }
Thomas Ming }

The Evidence being heard on the Tryal of Negroe **[Torn]** Judgment that the said Negro Cesar Be carried **[Torn]** Thursday the 24th of this Instant February and **[Torn]** Until he is Dead Between the Hours of Ten **[Torn]** the Forenoon, the said Negroe Cesar Valued **[Torn]** **[Entire line torn away]**.

Thos: Benbury   (Seal)   **[Torn]**
T. Barker   (Seal)   **[Torn]**
Willm. Bennett   (Seal)   **[Torn]**

I do Hereby Certify that the above   **[Torn]**
Copy of the Proceedings of the   **[Torn]**
Testimony whereof I have   **[Torn]**
hand and Affixed my Seal   **[Torn]**
twenty third day of February   **[Torn]**
                    Michl. Pay   **[Torn]**

Lowes Worley & Cullen Pollocks Claims

In House of Commons 22d Novr. 1785 on within & Mr Cabarrus recorded By Mr Blount referred to Commt. of Claims By Order J Hunt Clk
In the House of Commons 22 Novr. 1785
In Senate Nov. 22nd 1785 Referred as by the House of Commons By Order J. Haywood Clk
Allowed according to Law

****

North Carolina State Archives
Magistrates and Freeholders Courts, 1715-1793
Secretary of State Papers, Box #311

Secretary of State Papers
Magistrates Courts

Sam, a Slave

North Carolina }
Halifax County } Ss.

At a Court held agreeable to act of assembly for the Tryale of Slaves at the Courthouse in Halifax Town on Wednesday March Anno Dom. 1786

Present the Worshipfull
Nicholas Long   }
Good. Davis   } Esqrs. Justices &c.

John Kinchen   }
Anthony Hart   } Freeholders
Hance Bond   } &
William Gilmour   } Owners of Slaves

State No. Carolina   }
Negroe Sam the Property }
of John Lindsey   }

Tryed for Poisoning a Negroe Woman Named Sue belonging to Wm. Jackson. Guilty by the Court
Whereupon it is Ordered that the said Negroe Sam, be hanged by the Neck untill he be dead. And that the Sheriff of Halifax do Execution on the said Negroe Sam On Friday the 24th Instant, between the hours of twelve and two of the Clock in the Afternoon.

A True Copy
Test
L. Long   CC

Executed
Jno Geddy Shf.

Secretary of State Papers
Court Martial of lieut. William Lytle

Chapter Four

Court Martial

Lieut. William Lytle

North Carolina State Archives
Magistrates and Freeholders Courts, 1715-1793
Secretary of State Papers, Box #311

[Editor's Note: This is not a Magistrates Court Record. It is a Court Martial that was included in this box of records.]

Proceedings of a Court Martial held at Purisbury for the Trial of Lieut. Willm. Lytle of the No. Carolina Brigade Jany. 25th 1779

    The President Members & Judge Advocate being sworn The Judge Advocate prosecuting in the Name of the United State of America the Court proceeded to the trial of Lieut. Willm. Lytle who being in Arrest appears before the Court & the following Charge is exhibited against him Viz.   Disobedience of Orders

Lieut. Lytle pleads Not Guilty

    Capt. Armstrong being sworn says That he is acting Adjutant for Colo. Sumner's Regt. & that he warned Lieut. Lytle to mount Guard

Secretary of State Papers
Court Martial of lieut. William Lytle

under Capt. Jack one of the New Levy Capts. that Lieut. Lytle refused so to do sayin he wou'd not do duty under any of the New Levy Capts. who were Commissioned by the Governor of North Carolina agreeable to an Act of Assembly of said State to rank a Militia Captains & to receive the Pay Rations of Continental Captains.

  Lieut. Lytle being called upon to make his Defence assigns the following reasons for refusing to do duty at the time he was warned to mount guard by Capt. Armstrong, to wit, That he look'd upon the New Levy Captains as neither Continental or Militia Captains but that the State of North Carolina had exceeded the Authority delegated to them from Congress by annexing persons with the rank of Militia Captains to the Continental Battalions when they had already appointed Continental Captains to those Battalions raised in their State agreeable to the Authority vested in them by Congress.

  There was then laid before the Court an Act of Assembly of the State of North Carolina entitled An Act for raising Men to complete the Continental Battalions of this State - The 7th & 11th Clauses of which one as follows.

Clause 7th. And be it enacted by the Authority aforesaid That the men who shall be raised in manner aforesaid in the Districts of Halifax Edenton Newbern & Wilmington shall march to Halifax & from thence to Petersburg in Virginia & those who shall be raised in the Districts of Hillsborough & Salisbury shall rendeyvous at Peytonsburg in Pittsylvania with all possible expedition under the Command of such Continental Officer or Officers as the Commanding Officer in the Continental Service in this State shall appoint for that purpose & if there be none such Appointed in any County then the commanding Officer of the Militia in such County shall appoint a person to conduct the men thereto belonging either to Halifax or to Peytonsburg in Virginia as the Case may require there to be delivered to the Continental Officer appointed to receive them & such persons shall be allowed Captains pay & rations during the time of his employement & the men who shall be raised in manner aforesaid shall serve in the Continental Battalions of this State for the space of nine Months from the time that they shall arrive at either of the places aforesaid unless sooner discharged & shall be subject to the same Rules & Discipline & have the same pay & rations as the Continental troops from the day of their being voted in or enlisted.

Secretary of State Papers
Court Martial of lieut. William Lytle

Clause 11th. And be it enacted by the Authority aforesaid That the men raised in the Counties of Rowan & those men raised in the Counties of New Hanover & Brunswick shall elect one Captain Jointly in such Counties as raise more than fifty men the men so raised shall & may elect a Captain in every County & in such Counties which raise a smaller number than fifty the men shall & may elect one Lieutenant for every County & the persons so elected shall be commissioned accordingly by the Governor & shall march & continue with their respective Companies with the rank of militia & the pay & rations of regular Captains & Lieutenants during the time of their continuing Service.

A Resolve of Congress dated May 27th 1778 was also laid before the Court entitled the Establishment of the American Army Resolves in following words

In Congress May 27th 1778
Establishment of the American Army
1st. Infantry

Resolved that each Battalion of Infantry shall consist of nine Companies one of whom shall be of Light Infantry to be kept complete by Drafts from the Battalion & organized during the Campaigns into Corps of Light Infantry. --

That the Battalion consist of

		pay pr Month
1 Colo. & Capt.		75 Dollars
1 Lt. Colo. & Capt.		60
1 Major & Captain		50
6 Captains	each	40
1 Capt. Lieutenant		26 2/3
8 Lieutenants	each	26 2/3
9 Ensigns	each	20
1 Surgeon		60
1 Surgeons Mate		40
1 Sergt. Major		10
12 Msr. Sergeants		10
27 Sergeants	each	10

Secretary of State Papers
Court Martial of lieut. William Lytle

1 Drum Major	9	
1 Fife Major	9	
18 Drums & Fifes	7 1/3	
27 Corporals	7 1/3	
477 Privates	6 2/3	

Paymaster	} to be taken	} 20 Dolls.	} in addition to
Adjutant	} from the	} 13	} their pay as
Quarter Master	} line	} 13	} Officers of the line

Each of the Field Officers to command a Company
The Lieut. of the Colonels Company to have the rank of Captain Lieutenant.

In Consequence of the above Resolution there was another Resolve of Congress dated May 28th 1778 laid before the Court in the following words.

    Resolved that the Non-Commission'd Officers & other Men belonging to the Battalions of the State of No. Carolina now in Camp be forthwith reduced & formed by the Commander in Chief into as many Battalions as they will compleat according to the numbers composing the old battalion & that new formed battalions be officer'd agreeably to the new Arrangement of the Battalions & that all supernumerary Officers be immediately ordered to return to the State of North Carolina to officer the men raised by that State to complete their Quota of the Continental Battalions there to remain for the further order of Congress.

    Resolved that the State of North Carolina be required to fill up four Battalions & no more upon the new Establishment in addition to those now at Camp & to Officers the same with such of their Continental Officers as may be ordered from Camp as Supernumeraries of the Battalions there, or as are within the State of North Carolina or with such other persons as they shall think proper. And that the said four battalions remain within the State of North Carolina at such places as the Governor shall direct untill the further Order of Congress.

    Resolved, That the Officers who have been appointed by the State of North Carolina to battalions raised by that State & who shall not be anexed either to their battalions in Camp or to one of the said four Battalions shall not be considered as in the Service of these United States but as dismissed therefrom.

Secretary of State Papers
Court Martial of lieut. William Lytle

There was also laid before the Court a Report of a Joint Committee of the Senate & House of Commons of North Carolina which was concurred with by both Houses Augt. 14th 1778 in the following words.

The Joint Committee of both houses appointed to examine the several papers & make an arrangement of the Officers to command the battalions to be fitted up out of the New Levies in this State having & chosen General Persons Chairman beg leave to report as follows.

It appears to your Committee That in Consequence of orders from His Excellency the Governor A Board of Continental Officers hath been held at Halifax & Moor's Creek & have recommended Field Officers Captains & Subalterns to take the Command of the four Battalions to be filled out of the New Levies raised in Virtue of an Act of Assembly Which Arrangement & recommendation of the said board of Officers your Committee are of oppinion shoud take place & to which they beg Leave to refer.

Your Committee further report as their report that the Supernumerary Continental Officers remaining shou'd be discharged reserving to such reduced Officers the right of preferment according to rank whenever a Vacancy may happen & that the Militia Captains commanding the New Levies shall take rank & continue with their Companies agreeable to law unless when such Captains may have a less number than a full Company in which Case such Company to be Joined to others in the same Circumstance & one Captain to take Command This Arrangement to be made by the said Captains & the Men under their Command without the Interposition of the Continental Officers And that it is the Oppinion of your Committee that the said Captains of the said New raised Levies after such arrangement shall command Continental Lieutenants & have a right to sit in Court Martials on the trials of the said New raised Levies.

Your Committee have examined the returns of the New Levies now on duty from the districts of Salisbury & Hillsborough & have received Information that a Number also is now collected at Halifax & in Duplin County Upon the whole your Committee are of opinion that the New raised Levies together with such Continental Soldiers as are now in this State on duty are fully sufficient to complete the four battalions to be raised agreeable to the Resolve of the Continental Congress.

Secretary of State Papers
Court Martial of lieut. William Lytle

Which is Submitted

The House taking the said report into Consideration concurred therewith except that part reserving to such reduced Officers the Right of preferment according to rank whenever a vacancy may happen   By Order Jno. Hunt C.H.C.

In the Senate 14th Augt. 1778
Concurred with as altered by the Commons
Allen Jones S.S.

   Major Dixon being sworn says he was one of the Board of Officers held at Camp Moors Creek agreeable to a requisition of Governor Caswell. That four Battalions on the No. Carolina Establishment were then fully completed with Captains & Lieutenants from the Supernumerary Continental Officers returned from the Grand Army & those remaining in the State of No. Carolina That Lieut. Lytle was one of those Officers & was returned with the rank of Lieut. And that most of the Regular Lieutenants had rose in the Army from the Rank of Ensigns & had been recommended for their good Behaviours And further says that Jesse Steed a Sergeant ordered on the recruiting Service from the Continental Army appeared at Peytonsburg in the Character of a Captain of the New Levies from Chatham County.
   Major Dixon also said before the Court a return of the New Levies raised in Caswell County No. Carolina which was Delivered him by Colo. Saunders in which it appears that Capt. Robt. More one of the New Levy Captains was one of the Volunteers who turned out of Capt. John Moore's Company in said County.
Colo. Saunders being sworn says He was a Member of the Senate of No. Carolina at the Time the forgoing Report of the Joint Committee of both Houses was concurred with. That it appeared to him that it was the Idea of the Legislature & that the Expence of the New Levy Captains shou'd be paid by their own State & that a Question was put in the Joint Committee of both Houses whether the Continental Captains shou'd be dismissed & those raised on the New Establishment cintinued in the Continental Service which was determined in favour of Continental Captains. He further says that it was not intended by the Legislature that the New Levy Captains shou'd rise in the Continental line but is of opinion they were annexed to the Continental battalions in order to induce the men to enter

Secretary of State Papers
Court Martial of lieut. William Lytle

into the Service more chearfully Also that Capt. Robt. More when he turned out as a Volunteer received his Bounty as a private Soldier.

  Capt. Scull being sworn says He is lately returned from the Grand Army That the Devision of New Levies under Colo. Hogan had Joined part of the Grand Army & that the Captains chosen by them bore no rank & had no Command in the Army as he was inform'd by several Continental Officers belonging to the same Corps.

  The Court adjourned till tomorrow morning at 10 O'clock

Jany 26th 1779

  The Court met according to adjournment.

Capt. High being sworn says he had a Captains Commission in the New Levies which he produced in Court & was read as follows.

To Alsey Hight Gent. Greeting

We reposing especial Trust of Confidence in your Patriotism Valour Conduct & Fidelity do by these presents constitute & appoint you to be Captain of a Company of foot from the County of Wake to fill up the Continental Battalions You are therefore carefully & diligently to discharge the Duty of Captain by exercising & well disciplining the Officers & Soldiers under your Command & by doing & performing all manner of things thereunto belonging And we do strictly charge & require all Officers & Soldiers under your Command to be obedient to your Orders as Captain And you are to observe & follow such directions from time to time as you shall receive from your Superior Officer according to the Rules & Directions of Military Discipline & the Laws of this State.

  Witness Richd. Caswell Esqr. Captain General Governor & Commander in Chief in & over the said State under his hand & Seal at Arms at Newbern the 28th day of May Anno Dom: 1778 & in the second Year of our Independence   Rd. Caswell
By His Excellency's Command
Wm. Caswell pro Sec:

  Capt. Hight further sayeth That when he received the above Commission he was informed by the Colo. of Wake County who was a Member of the Assembly of No. Carolina that he was to march with his Company to the Northward but was to do no duty but receive the pay &

Secretary of State Papers
Court Martial of lieut. William Lytle

rations of a Continental Captain & return back with his men when their nine Months were expired. That he never understood he was to rise in the Continental line the only intentions of such Commissions being to induce the Men to enlist more chearfully into the Service And further sayeth That he did not imagine he was bound by the Articles of war for the better regulation of the Continental troops.

The Court adjourned till tomorrow morning at 10 o'clock

Jany. 27th 1779
The Court met according to adjournment.

General Rutherford being sworn sayeth That he does not know of any other resolve of Congress relative to raising the New Levies in North Carolina than that passed May 28th 1778 & that the Act of Assembly for raising the New Levies & appointing their Officers was passed in the Month of April or May preceeding Anterior to the Resolve of Congress That he does not know of any stipulation made by the Assembly with Congress for appointing any other Officers to the Levies than those mentioned in the Continental Arrangement but it was the Idea of himself & several members of the Senate that the New Levy Captains were to be paid by the Assembly of No. Carolina & that the measure was adopted for the more easily recruiting the Soldiers to fill up the Continental battalions & to induce them to march with the greater chearfulness to the army And further that he don't think that it was the Idea of any of the Members of the Assembly that those New Levy Captains shou'd rise in the Continental line That the Levies raised by Act of Assembly in April or May were directed to complete the four Battalions for the term of nine Months. Also that it was his Idea that the New Levy Captains shou'd be subject to all the disabilities & perform all the duties of Continental Captains. Colo. Lock being sworn sayeth That the New Levy Captains in Rowan County were Chosen from among the Soldiers after the ballot drafts & that Capt. Cowan received the bounty given for Volunteers from the Paymaster & also the Clothing allowed by Act of Assembly from his Company.

The Court adjourned till tomorrow morning at 10 O'clock

Jany. 28th 1779

Secretary of State Papers
Court Martial of lieut. William Lytle

The Court taking some time to examine & consider the proceedings had in this Cause adjourn till tomorrow morning at 10 O'Clock.

Jany. 29th 1779

The Court met according to adjournment. The Court having maturely deliberated on the matter before them conceive that although the Legislature of No. Carolina had an undoubted Authority from the Resolves of Congress to have Officer'd the Continental Battalions raised by that State with such persons as they thought most worthy to hold Commissions in them & to have rejected such Continental Officers as were ordered from the Grand Army as Supernumeraries of the Battalions there & also such as were before that time within the State of No. Carolina Yet as the Legislature did think proper by their Resolves of the 14th of last August to fill all the Commissions in the four additional Battalions raised by that State with such Continental field officers Captains & subalterns as were supernumeraries of the Battalions completed in the Grand Army the Court apprehend that this Act of Legislature was a full execution of the Power delegated to them by Congress & that as no Stipulations were made by them with Congress for Authority to annex any additional Officers to those Battalions all appointments by the State of a greater number of Officers than were Consistant with the Constitution of the Continental Army as far as such Appointments relate to the giving any Authority in those Battalions to such Officers are absolutely null & void. For that it was the Intention of Congress that no more than the Officers specified in their arrangement shou'd be annexed to the Continental Battalions of No. Carolina is evident to the Court, because, in their Resolve of the 28th May 1778 they determine that such New formed Battalions shall be officer'd agreeably to the new arrangement of the Battalions & that the Supernumerary Officers shou'd be ordered to return to No. Carolina to fill up four Battalions upon the New Establishment & actually dismiss from their Service all Officers heretofore appointed by the State of No. Carolina & not annexed to the Battalions in Camp or to one of the four thus raised & modelled agreeable to their New Arrangement. Now if Congress have thought it necessary to dismiss from their Service Officers of whose Patriotism Conduct Valour & Fidelity they had received the Strongest Proofs because their remaining with the new battalions wou'd be inconsistant with the Arrangement they had adopted It is not reasonable to suppose they wou'd allow other Officers of whom they have

Secretary of State Papers
Court Martial of lieut. William Lytle

had no experience to be annexed to those battalions particularly where their appointments wou'd be still more inconsistant with the late Constituted Arrangements & unprecedented in any army in the world. It is to be considered also that if one State without any particular agreement with Congress has a Right in itself to appoint two Captains to each Company in the Continental Battalions raised by that State another State may with equal Impropriety claim a right of annexing five Majors to each of their Continental Battalions & thus the United States instead of being possessed of a regular & well organized Army to defend their Liberties wou'd be perplexed with a variety of Army Constitutions & an unordinate unmilitary Chaos of battalions.

It is difficult to ascertain on what establishment these Officers are. They are certainly not Continental for they have not Continental Commissions neither is their Appointment consistant with the Resolutions or agreeable to the arrangements of Congress They are not strictly Militia for they have no Command over any Militia of the State which has appointed them nor are they annexed to any Militia Corps & however political the Intention of the State may have been in making these appointments in order to induce men to enter readily into the Service & to march with alacrity to & remain with chearfulness in the army yet in a Court Martial no political motives are to sway our determinations but the Evidence before us the Articles for the government of the forces of the United States & where the Articles are Silent our Conscience our best understanding & by the Customs of war are to guide our decisions The Court therefore for the reasons assigned above among many others, which must occur to every on the perusal of the proceedings had in this Cause are of opinion that the appointment & Commission of Capt. Jack may entitle him to receive from the State of No. Carolina the pay & Rations of a Captain as long as he shall continue with the Continental troops for which he was annexed yet he does not derive from Such appointment & commission and manner of command in or over the said troops & that Lieut. Lytle being a Continental officer regularly appointed to one of those battalions raised by No. Carolina on the New Establishment is Justified in refusing to do duty under him & is not guilty of any breach of the 5th Article of the 2d. Section of the Articles of war which punishes the Disobedience of any Lawful Command of a Superior Officer. Lieut. Lytle is therefore acquitted by the Court.

Appendix A
Table of Cases

Appendix A

Table of Cases

Cases

Andrew, a Slave [1783]
  Crime not given
  Executed
  Property of Miss Nancy Jones_____ 56

Annis, Phillis & Lucy, Slaves [1770]
  Murder
  Executed
  Annis, property of Henry Ormand
  Phillis, Property of Henry Ormand
  Lucy, Property of Wyrcott Ormand_____ 139

Arthur, a Slave [1785]
  Felony
  Executed
  Property of John Jones, Esqr._____ 151

Appendix A
Table of Cases

Bacchus, a Slave [1767]
   Rape
   Executed
   Property of Martha Hill _____ 27

Ben, a Slave [1766]
   Crime not given.
   Executed
   Property of Thomas Cook _____ 24

Boatswain, a Slave [1777]
   Outlawed & killed
   Property of Parker Quince _____ 46

Boston, a Slave [1767]
   Felony
   Executed
   Property of Richard Ward _____ 26

Cain, a Slave [1749]
   Murder
   Executed
   Property of James Baldwin _____ 109

Casar, a Slave [1770]
   Murder
   "Hanged by the Neck untill ... dead."
   Property of Mills reddick _____ 137

Cato & Peter, Slaves [1766]
   Crime not given.
   Executed
   Property of Elizabeth Bonner _____ 25

Cato, a Slave [1753]
   Attempted Murder
   "Guilty of Death."
   Property of Isaac Jones _____ 112

Appendix A
Table of Cases

Cato, a Slave [1762]
  Runaway & Outlawed
  Shot while being apprehended
  Died in jail.
  Property of Richard Spaight, Esqr. _____ 17

Cato, a Slave [1766]
  Rape
  "Fastened to a Stake & there Burnt untill he be dead."
  Property of the Estate of Henry Bonner _____ 119

Cato, a Slave [1768]
  Felony
  Burned to death
  Owner not named _____ 31

Cato, a Slave [1785]
  Murder
  "Hanged by the Neck untill Dead ... head be severed from his Body and Stuck on a pole."
  Property of William Powell _____ 153

Cesar, a Slave [1762]
  Murder
  Executed
  Property of the Estate of James Parker _____ 18

Charles, a Slave [1759]
  Felony, (Stealing)
  "Hanged by the Neck untill his Body is Dead."
  Property of William Pratt _____ 12

Charles, a Slave [1766]
  Crime not given.
  Castrated
  Property of Samuel Duncomb _____ 24

Appendix A
Table of Cases

Cudjo, a Slave [1767]
　Felony
　Executed
　Property of the Admrs. of Francis Corbin _____ 27

Cudjo, a Slave [1768]
　Runaway & Outlawed
　Drownded while escaping
　Property of William Campbell, Esqr. _____ 131

Cudjoe, a Slave [1768]
　Outlawed & Drownded
　Property of William Campbell _____ 30

Cuff, a Slave [1770]
　Assisting in a Murder
　Executed
　Property of Henry Ormand _____ 140

Cuff, a Slave [1770]
　Suspicion of Poisoning
　"Hang'd by the Neck ... until he is dead."
　Property of the Estate of Benjamin Ward _____ 135

Cyrus & Sampson, Slaves [1761]
　Crime not given.
　Castrated
　Cyrus, the property of Darby Eugan
　Sampson, the property of Job How _____ 15

Davie, a Slave
　Felony
　Executed
　Property of Isaac Nichols _____ 10

Dick, a Slave [1764]
　Poisoning another Negroe.

Appendix A
Table of Cases

Hanged
Property of Hezekiah Russ _____ 20

Dick, a Slave [1767]
  Murder
  Executed
  Property of Thomas Edwards _____ 26

Dick, a Slave [1768]
  Attempted Murder
  "Hung by the Neck untill he is dead...his Head to be Choped off and put up at the Forks of the Road."
  Property of John Brevard _____ 122

Dublin, a Slave [1762]
  Murder
  Executed
  Property of the Estate of Thomas Corprew _____ 19

Essex, a Slave [1740]
  Felony
  Executed
  Property of Thomas Barker _____ 10

Esther, a Slave [1779]
  Attempted Poisoning
  Executed
  Property of James Blount _____ 76

Esther, a Slave [1786]
  Poisoning her Mistress
  "Hanged by the Neck untill she be dead."
  Property of James Blount _____ 148

Galloway, a Slave [1780]
  Outlawed & Killed
  Property of John Walker _____ 91

Appendix A
Table of Cases

George, a Slave [1751]
  Felony
  Executed
  Property of John Macon _____ 11

George, a Slave [1770]
  Rape
  "Hang'd by the Neck untill he be dead ... his head to be Severed from his Body and Stuck up at the Forks of the Road.
  Property of James Moore _____ 138

Gibby, a Slave [1777]
  Murder
  "Hanged till he was dead dead dead ... head cut off and Stuck upon a pole."
  Property of Samuell Dwight _____ 144

Hannah, a Slave [1782]
  Attempting to poison her Master
  Executed
  Property of John Green _____ 54

Harry, a Slave [1768]
  Felony
  Executed
  Property of Colo. Wilson Cary _____ 31

Hercules & Cesar, Slaves [1780]
  Felony
  Executed
  Hercules, property of Lois Worley
  Cesar, Property of [?] _____ 155

Isaac, a Slave [1777]
  Murder
  "Burnt alive."
  Property of Mrs. Dupree _____ 144

Appendix A
Table of Cases

Ismael, a Slave [1745]
   Felony
   "Judgment of Death to be Hanged." _____ 105

Jack & Stephen, Slaves [1748]
   Felony & "Braking out of the Goal."
   Stephen to be Hanged
   Stephen, property of William Sparrel
   Jack, property of Edward Howcalt _____ 106

Jack, a Slave [1761]
   Runaway & Felony
   Shot while a Runaway
   Property of John Dalrymple _____ 14

Jack, a Slave [1762]
   Crime not given.
   Castrated
   Property of Joshua Bodiley _____ 17

Jack, a Slave [1762]
   Felony
   Executed
   Property of John Roberts _____ 16

Jack, a Slave [1768]
   Felony
   Executed
   Property of Ezekiel Moore _____ 28

Jack, a Slave [1768]
   Robbery
   "Hang'd by the Neck until he is dead."
   Property of John Corbyn _____ 127

Jack, a Slave [1778]
   Horse Stealing

Appendix A
Table of Cases

Executed
Property of Philip Reaford _____ 91

Jack, a Slave [1781]
Giving out Poison
Executed
Property of William Eaton _____ 67

Jack, a Slave [1781]
Inciting other Slaves to poison their Masters
Executed
Property of Col. William Eaton _____ 54

Jacob, a Slave [1783]
Felony
Hanged
Property of William West _____ 66

James, a Slave [1779]
Murder
Executed
Property of Sarah Dupree _____ 48

Jamy, a Slave [1778]
Murder
Burned to death
Property of Sarah Dupree _____ 86

Jemmy, a Slave [1762]
Crime not given.
Castrated & Executed
Property of Thomas Jones _____ 19

Jemmy, a Slave [1762]
Felony
Executed
Property of Thomas Jones _____ 18

Appendix A
Table of Cases

Jim, a Slave [1777]
  Stealing
  "Hanged by the Neck untill he be dead."
  Property of Benjamin Clark _____ 145

Jim, a Slave [1779]
  Felony (Stealing)
  Executed
  Property of Benjamin Clark _____ 47

Jim, a Slave [1783]
  Murder
  Hanged
  Property of Lovelace Savage _____ 68

Joe, a Slave [1764]
  Crime not given.
  Castrated
  Property of James Jeter _____ 20

John Brown, a Slave [1768]
  Imprisoned & Released
  Owner not named. _____ 28

Johnney, a Slave [1768]
  Crime not given
  Executed
  Property of James Hasell, Junr. _____ 30

Johnny, a Slave [1768]
  Robbery
  "Hang'd by the Neck untill he is dead...and his head to be affixed upon the New Road."
  Property of James Harrell, Junr. _____ 126

Josey, a Slave [1744]
  Runaway & Shot
  Property of Job Howe _____ 104

Appendix A
Table of Cases

Limerick, a Slave [1787]
  Crime not given
  Executed
  Property of Col. Grant ... 86

London, a Slave [1766]
  Outlawed, apprehended & drownded
  Property of Lewis Henry De Rosset ... 22

Luke, a Slave [1766]
  Crime not given.
  Executed
  Property of John Cherry ... 22

Lymus, a Slave [1786]
  Outlawed & Shot
  Property of Samuel Clegg ... 70

Morrise, a Slave [1762]
  Murder
  Burned to death
  Property of William Peacock ... 17

Ned & Daniel, Slaves [1768]
  Felony (Suspicion of Poisoning)
  "Hanging them by the Neck till Each of them be dead."
  Ned, the property of John Thornton
  Daniel, the property of William Williamson ... 129

Nedd, a Slave [1741]
  Felony (Burglary)
  Executed
  Property of William Hoskins ... 10

Negroe fellow, a Slave [1761]
  Crime not given.
  Burned to death
  Owner's name not stated. ... 15

Appendix A
Table of Cases

Negroe Slave [1767]
  Crime not given.
  Castrated
  Property of Elizabeth Flemming _____ 27

Peter & Essex, Slaves [1769]
  Capital Crimes
  "Executed by hanging by the Neck till they were dead."
  Property of Richard Brownrigg, Esqr. _____ 134

Peter, a Slave [1757]
  Burglary & Felony
  "Said Negroe to be hanged."
  Property of John MacKenzie _____ 115

Peter, a Slave [1786]
  Murder
  Executed
  Property of Moore Wright _____ 70

Phill, a Slave [1743]
  Rape
  "Hanged till he is dead & then his private parts Cut off & Thrown in his face." _____ 102

Phillis, a Slave [1768]
  Runaway, Outlawed & shot
  Property of James Hassell, Esqr. _____ 29

Phoebe & Mary, Slaves [1757]
  Crime not named
  Phoebe, "to Receive fifty Lashes well laid on her bare back."
  Mary, 'to be hanged by the Neck."
  Phoebe, property of Mrs. McCorkel
  Mary, property of Ralph Taylor _____ 116

Pompey, a Slave [1765]
  Attempted Murder

Appendix A
Table of Cases

"Hanged by the Neck till he shall be dead, And that his Head shall be Severed from his Body, And Stuck up on a Stake."
Property of Richard Yeates_____ 120

Pompey, a Slave [1766]
  Felony
  Executed
  Property of Richard Yates _____ 21

Prince, a Slave [1751]
  Crime not given.
  "Sentenced to Death."
  Property of Richard Grise_____ 111

Prince, a Slave [1783]
  Crime not given.
  Executed
  Property of Robert Jarmain _____ 150

Quamino, a Slave [1768]
  Felony
  Executed
  Property of the Exrs. of John Duboise _____ 29

Quamino, a Slave [1768]
  Robbery
  "Hang'd by the Neck until he is dead."
  Property of the Estate of John Duboise _____ 125

Quash, a Slave [1767]
  Murder
  Executed
  Property of George Campbell _____ 28

Quash, a Slave [1767]
  Murder of a Negroe man
  "Hanged by the Neck til he be Dead."
  Property of George Campbell_____ 123

Appendix A
Table of Cases

Quaugh, a Slave [1761]
  Crime not given.
  Castrated
  Property of Mr. Dry _____ 15

Robin, Jack & Jemmy, Slaves [1768]
  Murder
  Executed
  Property of the Exrs. of Samuel Thomas _____ 29

Rose, a Slave [1766]
  House Burning
  Executed
  Property of the Estate of Matthew Raboun _____ 21

Sam, a Slave [1764]
  Crime not given.
  Castrated
  Property of the Estate of Capt. Buck _____ 21

Sam, A Slave [1786]
  Crime not given
  Executed
  Property of John Lindsay _____ 69

Sam, a Slave [1786]
  Poisoning a Negroe Woman
  Executed
  Owner not named _____ 70

Sam, a Slave [1786]
  Poisoning another Slave
  "Hanged by the Neck untill he is dead."
  Property of John Lindsey _____ 157

Sambo, a Slave [1762]
  Crime not given.

Appendix A
Table of Cases

Castrated
Property of Edward Williams _____ 18

Scipio, a Slave [1741]
  Murder
  Burned to Death
  Property of Bartholomew Evans _____ 101

Seip, a Slave [1771]
  Felony (Burglary)
  "Hanged by the Neck untill he be Dead."
  Property of James Coor _____ 141

Serina, a Slave [1752]
  Felony (Stealing)
  Executed
  Property of Solomon King _____ 111

Simon, a Slave [1766]
  Crime not given.
  Executed
  Property of Alexander Grant _____ 23

Simon, a Slave [1767]
  Murder
  Executed
  Property of William Cannon _____ 25

Simon, a Slave [1779]
  Felony
  Executed
  Property of Benjamin Hix of South Carolina _____ 149

Simon, a Slave [1786]
  Felony
  Executed
  Property of Benjamin Hicks _____ 70

Appendix A
Table of Cases

Slave, not named [1768]
  Felony
  Executed
  Property of William Salter _____ 30

Slave, not named [1771]
  Murder
  Executed
  Property of Robert Howe _____ 34

Slave, not Named [1777]
  Felony
  "Condemned & Hanged"
  Property of Thomas McLin _____ 45

Slave, not named [1777]
  Outlawed & killed
  Property of Robert Gibbs _____ 45

Slave, not named [1782]
  Felony
  Executed
  Property of John Kindred _____ 69

Slave, not named [1783]
  Runaway & killed
  Property of William Bryan _____ 57

Slave, not named [1786]
  Crime not given
  Executed
  Owner not named _____ 78

Swift, a Slave [1783]
  Felony (Stealing)
  "Hanged by the neck until he was dead."
  Property of Elijah Graves _____ 62

Appendix A
Table of Cases

Tartola Prince, a Slave [1781]
  Outlawed & killed
    Property of William Bryan, Esqr. _____ 51

Titus, a Slave [1764]
  Outlawed and shot.
    Property of the Executors of John Daniel _____ 20

Titus, a Slave [1777]
  Rape
  "Hanged by the Neck till he is Dead, then his Body to be Burnt."
    Property of John Evans _____ 146

Toddy & Moses, Slaves [1766]
  Crime not given.
    Property of Cullen Pollock _____ 23

Tom, a Slave [1755]
  Felony (Stealing)
  "Castrated by having both his Stones Cut out."
    Property of John Duboise _____ 113

Tom, a Slave [1755]
  Felony
  Executed
    Property of Captain John DuBois _____ 11

Tom, a Slave [1761]
  Crime not given.
  Executed
    Property of Joseph Watters _____ 14

Tom, a Slave [1762]
  Crime not given.
  Castrated & died.
    Property of John Oliver _____ 16

Appendix A
Table of Cases

Tom, a Slave [1762]
  Crime not given.
  Castrated
  Property of James Long_____ 17

Tom, a Slave [1763]
  Felony
  Sentence not given.
  Property of Stephen Wright _____ 117

Tom, a Slave [1784]
  Felony
  Executed
  Property of Isaac Jordain _____ 65

Tonay, a Slave [1787]
  Felony (Robbery)
  Hanged
  Property of Thomas Harvey _____ 85

Toney, a Slave [1769]
  Felony & Robbery
  "Hang'd by the Neck untill he shall be Dead."
  Property of Francis Clayton _____ 132

Toney, a Slave [1777]
  Murder
  "Burnt alive."
  Property of Peter Allston_____ 145

Toney, a Slave [1785]
  Murder
  "Chained to a Stake there to be Burnt to Death."
  Property of the Estate of George Gibbs_____ 152

Tony, a Slave [1756]
  Runaway

179

Appendix A
Table of Cases

Killed while being apprehended.
Property of George Moore, Esqr. _____ 11

Tony, a Slave [1783]
  Outlawed & killed
  Property of Joseph Locke _____ 63

Two Negroe Slaves [1764]
  Crime not given.
  Castrated
  One the property of John Duboise
  The other the property of Doctor Corbyn _____ 19

Will, a slave [1739]
  Felony (Stealing)
  "Hanged by the Neck till he be dead." _____ 9

Will, a Slave [1748]
  Felony
  "Sentence of Death."
  Property of George Kornegue _____ 108

Will, a Slave [1768]
  Murder
  "Hung alive in Gibbets at the Gallows."
  Property of Bryant Lee _____ 128

Will, a Slave [1771]
  Threatening to Poison
  "Apprehended the said Negroe ... thereafter, died in the custody of the Constable."
  Property of Elizabeth Blaning _____ 133

Appendix B
North Carolina Laws

Appendix B

North Carolina Laws

STATE RECORDS OF NORTH CAROLINA
VOLUME XXIII., 1715-1776
EDITED BY: WALTER CLARK
NASH BROTHERS BOOK AND JOB PRINTERS
GOLDSBORO, NORTH CAROLINA, 1904

CHAPTER XLVI.
1715. An Act Concerning Servants & Slaves. (Repealed by Act 4 April, 1741, ch. 24.). (Pages 62-66).

XI. And Be It Further Enacted by the Authority afors'd that where any slave shall be guilty of any Crime or Offence whatsoever the same shall be heard & determined by any three Justices of the Precinct Court where such Offence or Crime shall be Committed & three Freeholders such as have Slaves in that Precinct or the Major part of them shall have full power & authority & they are hereby required & commanded to Trye the same according to their best Judgment & Discretion at such time & place as the first in Commission in the said precinct shall appoint & to pass Judgment for life or Member or any other Corporal Punishment on such Offender & cause Execution of the same Judgment to be made & done. And if any Slave shall be killed in apprehending or that shall by Judgment of the said Justices & Freeholders shall give a Certificate of Value of such Slave under their hands to the

Appendix B
North Carolina Laws

Master or Owner of such Slave who shall be thereby Entitulled to a Poll-Tax on all Slaves in the Government to make up that sum to the Owner of such Slave so publickly Executed or killed in Apprehending.

****

THE STATE RECORDS OF NORTH CAROLINA
VOLUME XXV., SUPPLEMENT, 1669-1771
EDITED BY: WALTER CLARK
NASH BROTHERS BOOK AND JOB PRINTERS
GOLDSBORO, N.C., 1906

CHAPTER V.
1720. An Act in Explanation of an Act Concerning Servants and Slaves. (Pages 169-170).
Whereas, the Special Court appointed by the Said Act for the Tryall of Slaves have power thereby Granted them against Slaves convicted before them to pass Judgm't for Life Member or other Corporal punishments, and it hath been ascerted that power is thereby granted to the Said Court if they see Cause to give Judgm't for the imprisoning any Slave, deeming it a Corporal punishment, and inasmuch as the imprisoning a Slave is an apparant Damage and Loss to the Master,

I. Be it therefore Enacted by his Excellency, the palatin and the rest of the true and absolute Lords Prop'ts of Carolina, by and with the Advice and Consent of the Rest of the Members of the General Assembly not met at the General Court House at Queen Anne's Creek in Chowan precinct for the N'o. East Part of the Said Province, and it is hereby Enacted, That Corporal punishments in that Case shall not be Construed to extend or include Inprisonment of the Offender, nor shall any such Judgment of the said Court hereafter to be passed, be good or Execution thereof be done.

****

THE STATE RECORDS OF NORTH CAROLINA
VOLUME XXIII., 1715-1776
EDITED BY: WALTER L. CLARK
NASH BROTHERS BOOK AND JOB PRINTERS

Appendix B
North Carolina Laws

GOLDSBORO, N.C., 1904

CHAPTER XXIV.
1741. An Act Concerning Servants and Slaves. (Pages 191-204).

XLV. And whereas many Times Slaves run away and lie out hid and lurking in the Swamps, Woods and other Obscure Places, killing Cattle and Hogs, and committing other Injuries to the Inhabitants in this Government: Be it therefore Enacted, by the Authority aforesaid, That in all such Cases, upon Intelligence of any Slave or Slaves lying out as aforesaid, any Two Justices of the Peace for the County wherein such Slave or Slaves is or are supposed to lurk to do Mischief, shall, and they are hereby impowered and required, to issue Proclamation against such Slave or Slaves (reciting his or their Name or Names, and the Name or Names of their Owner or Owners, if known), thereby requiring him or them, and every of them, forthwith to surrender him or themselves; and also, to impower and require the Sheriff of the said County to take such Power with him as he shall think fit and necessary for going in search and pursuit of and effectual apprehending such outlying Slave or Slaves; which Proclamation shall be published on a Sabbath Day, at the Door of every Church or Chappel, or for want of such, at the Place where Divine Service shall be performed in the said County, by the Parish Clerk or Reader, immediately after Divine Service: And if any Slave or Slaves against whom Proclamation hath been thus issued, stay out and do not immediately return home, it shall be lawful for any Person or Persons whatsoever to kill and destroy such Slave or Slaves by such Ways and Means as he or she shall think fit, without Accusation or Impeachment of any Crime for the same.

XLVI. Provided always, and it is further Enacted, that for every Slave killed in Pursuance of this Act, or put to Death by Law, the Master or Owner of such Slave shall be paid by the Public; and all Tryals of Slaves for Capital or other Crimes, shall be in the Manner and according as hereinafter is directed.

XLVII. And be it further Enacted, by the Authority aforesaid, That if any Number of Negroes or other Slaves, that is to say, Three or more, shall at any Time hereafter, consult, advise or conspire to rebell, or make insurrection, or shall plot or conspire the Murther of any Person or Persons whatsoever, every such consulting, plotting, or conspiring, shall

Appendix B
North Carolina Laws

be adjudged and deemed Felony; And the Slave or Slaves convicted thereof, in Manner hereafter directed, shall suffer Death.

XLVIII. And be further Enacted, by the Authority aforesaid, That every Slave committing such Offence, or any other Crime or Misdemeanor, shall forthwith be committed, by any Justice of the Peace, to the Common Gaol of the County within which the said Offence shall be committed, there to be safely kept; and that the Sheriff of such County, upon such Commitment, shall forthwith Certify the same to any Justice in the Commission for the said Court, for the Time being, resident in the County, who is thereupon required and directed to issue a Summons for Two or more Justices of the said Court, and Four Freeholders, such as shall have Slaves in the said County; which said Three Justices, and Four Freeholder Owners of Slaves, are hereby impowered and required, upon Oath, to try all Manner of Crimes and Offences that shall be committed by any Slave or Slaves, at the Court House of the County, and to take for Evidence the Confession of the Offender, the Oath of one or more credible Witnesses, or such Testimony of Negroes, Mulattoes or Indians, bond or free, with pregnant Circumstances, as to them shall seem convincing without the Solemnity of a Jury; and the Offender being then found guilty, to pass such Judgment upon such Offender, according to their Discretion, as the Nature of the Crime or Offence shall require; and on such Judgment, to award Execution.

XLIX. Provided always, and be it Enacted, That it shall and may be lawful for each and every Justice, being in the Commission of the Peace for the County where any Slave or Slaves shall be tried, by Virtue of this Act (who is Owner of Slaves), to set up such Tryal, and act as a Member of such Court, tho' he or they be not summoned thereto: Anything before herein contained to the Contrary, in any wise, notwithstanding.

L. And to the End such Negro, Mulatto or Indian, bond or free, not being Christians, as shall hereafter be produced as an Evidence on the Tryal of any Slave or Slaves for Capital or other Crimes, may be under the greater Obligation to declare the Truth; Be it further Enacted, That where any such Negro, Mulatto or Indian, bond or free, shall, upon due Proof made, or pregnant Circumstances, appearing before any County Court within this Government, be found to have given False Testimony, every such Offender shall, without further Tryal, be ordered by the said Court to have one Ear nailed to the Pillory, and there stand for the Space

Appendix B
North Carolina Laws

of One Hour, and the said Ear to be cut off, and thereafter the other Ear nailed in like manner, and cut off, at the Expiration of one other Hour; and moreover, to order every such Offender Thirty Nine Lashes well laid on, on his or her bare Back, at the common whipping Post.

LI. And be it further Enacted, by the Authority aforesaid, That at every such Tryal of Slaves committing Capital or other Offences, the first Person in Commission setting on such Tryal shall, before the Examination of every Negro, mulatto or Indian, not being a Christian, charge such to declare the Truth.

LII. Provided Always, and it is hereby intended, That the Master, Owner or Overseer of any Slave, to be arraigned and tryed by Virtue of this Act, may appear at the Tryal and make what just Defence he can for such Slave or Slaves; so that such Defence do not relate to any Formality in the Proceeding on the Tryal.

LIII. And be it further Enacted, by the Authority aforesaid, That when any Slave shall be convicted Capitally by Virtue of this Act, the Justices and Freeholders that shall sit on such Tryals, shall put a Valuation, in Proclamation Money, upon such Slave so convicted, and Certify under their Hands and Seals, such Valuation to the next Assembly; that the said Assembly may make suitable Allowance thereupon, to the Master or Owner of such Slave.

LIV. And be it further Enacted, by the Authority aforesaid, That if in the dispersing any unlawful Assemblies of rebel Slaves or Conspirators, or seizing the Arms and Ammunition of such as are prohibited by this Act to keep the same, or in apprehending Runaways, or in Correction by Order of the County Court, any Slave shall happen to be killed or destroyed, the Court of the County where such Slave shall be killed, upon Application of the Owner of such Slave, and due Proof thereof made, shall put a Valuation, in Proclamation Money, upon such Slave so killed, and certify such Valuation to the next Session of Assembly; that the said Assembly may make suitable Allowance thereupon, to the Master or Owner of such Slave.

LV. Provided always, and be it further Enacted, That nothing herein contained, shall be construed, deemed or taken, to defeat or bar the Action of any Person or Persons, whose Slave or Slaves shall happen to be killed by any other Person whosoever, contrary to the Directions and true Intent and Meaning of this Act; but that all and every Owner or Owners of

Appendix B
North Carolina Laws

such Slave or Slaves, shall and may bring his, her or their Action for Recovery of Damages for such Slave or Slaves so killed.

CHAPTER VI.
1753. An additional Act to an Act concerning servants and slaves. (Pages 388-390).

IX. And be it further Enacted, by the authority aforesaid, That if any Slave or Slaves shall be killed on outlawry, or shall commit any Crime or Misdemeanor for which, he, she, or they, shall be capitally convicted, the Owner of such Slave or Slaves so outlawed or executed, shall be debarred all claim on the Public for the Value of such Slave or Slaves, and the Justices of the County Court and Freeholders, who shall value the Slave or Slaves so killed, or sit on the Trial of such Slave or Slaves so capitally convicted, shall not make any certificate of the value of the same, unless it shall be made appear, on Motion for such Certificate, by the Owner, or some other Person, that such Slave or Slaves, killed on outlawry, or capitally convicted, shall have been sufficiently cloathed, and shall likewise have constantly received, for the preceeding Year, an Allowance not less than a Quart of Corn per Diem.

X. And be it Enacted, by the authority aforesaid, That in case any Slave or Slaves, who shall not appear to have been cloathed and fed according to the Intent and Meaning of this Act, shall be convicted of stealing any Corn, Cattle, Hogs, or other Goods whatsoever, from any Person not the owner of such Slave or Slaves, such injured Person shall and may maintain an Action of Trespass against the Master, Owner, or Possessor of such Slave, in the General or County Court, and shall recover his or her Damages, with Costs of Suit; any Law, Usage, or Custom, to the contrary notwithstanding.

****

STATE RECORDS OF NORTH CAROLINA
VOLUME XXIII., 1715-1776
EDITED BY: WALTER CLARK
NASH BROTHERS BOOK AND JOB PRINTERS
GOLDSBORO, NORTH CAROLINA, 1904

CHAPTER VII.

Appendix B
North Carolina Laws

1758. An additional Act, intituled, An Act concerning Servants and Slaves. (Pages 488-489).

    I. Whereas many great Charges have arisen to the Province by Punishment of Slaves, who having Liberty from their Owners to hire themselves out, and having committed Robberies; by the Importation of Slaves from Foreign Parts for Crimes by them committed; by the condemnation of Slaves to Death for capital Crimes, for want of a punishment adequate to the Crimes they have been guilty of; and by the high Valuation of Slaves condemned to Death, or killed by Virtue of an Outlawry;

    II. Be it Enacted, by the Governor, Council, and Assembly, and by the authority of the same, That no Person who shall Permit any Slave to hire himself or herself out, shall be intitled to receive any Pay from the Public, should they be punished for any Crimes by them committed during the Time of such Permission; any Usage or Custom, to the contrary, notwithstanding.

    III. And be it further Enacted, by the Authority aforesaid, That no Person hereafter purchasing any Slave, transported for Crimes from foreign Parts, into this Province, shall be intitled to receive any Payment from the Public, should such Slave afterwards be convicted and punished for any Crimes committed within this Province; unless he first make Oath, in the Court appointed for trying such Slave, that he did not at the Time of his purchasing, know that such Slave had been transported here for any Crimes committed in Foreign Parts.

    IV. And be it further Enacted, by the Authority aforesaid, That no male Slave shall for the First Offence, be condemned to Death, unless for Murder or Rape; but for every other Capital Crime, shall for the First Offence, suffer castration, which punishment every Court trying such Slave, shall be impowered, and are hereby directed to cause to, be inflicted; and the Sheriff shall cause such Judgment to be duly Executed; for which he shall have and receive, from the Public, Twenty Shillings, Proclamation Money, and no more; any Usage or Custom to the contrary, notwithstanding.

    V. Provided always, That such Slave be valued by the Court Trying him, in the Usual Manner, that in case Death should ensue the Owner might be paid by the Public; and that the Sum of Three Pounds, Proclamation Money, shall be allowed and paid by the Public, to defray the expence of the Cure, of each Slave Castrated.

Appendix B
North Carolina Laws

VI. And be it further Enacted, by the Authority aforesaid, That there shall not be allowed by the Public to the owner of any Slave which shall hereafter happen to be convicted of any Capital Offence, killed on outlawry, or in being apprehended when run away, more than the Sum of Sixty Pounds, Proclamation Money; any Law or Custom to the contrary, notwithstanding.

****

THE STATE RECORDS OF NORTH CAROLINA
VOLUME XXIII., 1715-1776
EDITED BY: WALTER CLARK
NASH BROTHERS BOOK AND JOB PRINTERS
GOLDSBORO, NORTH CAROLINA, 1904

Chapter VIII.
1764. An Act to amend An Act therein mentioned, concerning Servants and Slaves. (Page 656).
I. Whereas by the Fourth, Fifth, and Sixth Sections of an Act of Assembly of this Province, passed in the Year of our Lord One Thousand Seven Hundred and Fifty Eight, intituled, an Additional Act to an Act Intituled, An Act concerning Servants and Slaves, it is Enacted, That no male Slave Shall, for the First Offence, be condemned to Death, unless for Murder or Rape; but for every other Capital Crime, shall, for the First Offence, suffer Castration; and that the Court trying such Slave shall value the same:
II. Be it Enacted, by the Governor, Council, and Assembly, and it is hereby Enacted, by the Authority of the same, That the Fourth, Fifth, and Sixth Sections of the aforesaid Act be, and are hereby, repealed and made void.
III. And be it further Enacted, by the Authority aforesaid, That there shall not be allowed by the Public to the Owner of any Slave who shall hereafter be executed in Virtue of the Judgment of the Court who shall try such Slave, any larger Sum than Eighty Pounds, Proclamation Money; any Law, Usage, or Custom to the Contrary notwithstanding.

****

Appendix B
North Carolina Laws

THE STATE RECORDS OF NORTH CAROLINA
VOLUME XXIV
LAWS 1777-1788
EDITED BY: WALTER CLARK
NASH BROTHERS BOOK AND JOB PRINTERS
GOLDSBORO, N.C., 1906

CHAPTER XII. 2ND SESSION.
1779. An Act to amend an Act, intituled, An Act concerning servants and slaves. (Pages 282-283).

I. Whereas from the present very small and inadequate allowance by the public to the owners of executed slaves, crimes and thefts by them committed go frequently unpunished, such slaves being screened from public justice often by their owners;

II. Be it therefore enacted by the General Assembly of the State of North Carolina, and it is hereby enacted by the authority of the same, that there shall not be allowed by the public to the owner of any slave who shall hereafter be executed in virtue of the judgment of the court who shall try such slave, any larger sum than seven hundred pounds current money for a prime slave, and so in proportion for slaves of a less value; any law, usage or custom, to the contrary, notwithstanding.

III. And be it further enacted by the authority aforesaid, that so much of the before recited act as comes within the purview and meaning of this act, shall be, and the same is hereby repealed and made void.

CHAPTER X. 3RD SESSIONS.
1781. An additional Act to an Act, intitled, An Act concerning Servants and Slaves. (Pages 382-383).

I. Forasmuch as by the laws of this State in all cases whatsoever where a slave has been guilty of a criminal offence which inflicts the punishment of death, and is tried and convicted thereof, many poor widows, orphan children, and other good citizens of this State, may be deprived of their chief, and perhaps only support, as the allowances heretofore made by law can in no case exceed the sum of seven hundred pounds: For remedy whereof:

II. Be it enacted by the General Assembly of the State of North Carolina, and it is hereby enacted by the authority of the same, that when a slave shall hereafter be guilty of a criminal offence, for which such slave

Appendix B
North Carolina Laws

shall be condemned to suffer death, the court before whom the trial shall happen are hereby required to certify in writing under their hands, the value of the slave in the currency of the State at the time of the trial; and the owner of the slave so condemned and executed shall be intitled to the one half of such valuation, to be paid out of the public treasury of this State, any custom or law to the contrary notwithstanding.

CHAPTER XIV. 1ST SESSION.
1783. An Act to amend an Act passed in the year of our Lord, one thousand seven hundred and forty one, intituled, An Act concerning Servants and Slaves. (Pages 496-497).

I. Whereas the mode directed in the said Act for thr trial of slaves where the offence may be of a small and trivial nature is found to be attended with delay, great loss of time, and expence to the owner; For remedy whereof,

II. Be it therefore enacted by the General Assembly of the State of North Carolina, and it is hereby enacted by the authority of the same, That where any slave or slaves shall hereafter committ any misdemeanor or offence which is not by law declared capital, and which in the opinion of the justice or justices before whom such offending slave may be carried for examination, shall appear to be of so trivial a nature as not to deserve a greater punishment than a single justice of the peace is by this Act impowered to inflict, such justice shall, and he is hereby authorised and impowered forthwith to issue subpoenas if necessary, to compell the attendance of witnesses, and proceed immediately upon the trial of such slave in a summary way, and to pass sentence and award execution; provided the punishment extends no further than by ordering the offender to be publicly whipped not exceeding forty lashes: And where the offence for which any slave shall be apprehended shall appear to the justice or justices to be of such nature as to deserve any other or greater punishment, such offending slave shall be committed to gaol, and stand his or her trial by a court in the way prescribed by the afore recited Act.

III. Provided, That upon all trials of slaves before any justice of the peace, for any misdemeanor under this Act, any other of the justices of the county where such slave may be upon trial, may, if they think proper, sit upon and assist in the examination and trial.

CHAPTER XVII. 1ST SESSION.

Appendix B
North Carolina Laws

1786. An Act to Repeal the Several Acts of Assembly Respecting Slaves Within This State, as far as the Same Relates to Making an Allowance to the Owner or Owners for any Executed or Outlawed Slave or Slaves. (Page 809).

Whereas many persons by cruel treatment to their slaves, cause them to commit crimes for which many of the said slaves are executed, whereby a very burdensome debt is unjustly imposed on the good citizens of this State: For remedy whereof,

I. Be it Enacted by the General Assembly of the State of North Carolina, and it is Enacted by the authority of the same, That from and after the passing of this Act, the several Acts of Assembly of this State, as far as relates to making an allowance for any outlawed or executed slave or slaves, shall be, and the same is hereby repealed and made utterly void. (Passed Jan. 6, 1787.)

****

LAWS OF THE STATE OF NORTH CAROLINA
REVISED, UNDER THE AUTHORITY OF THE GENERAL ASSEMBLY
VOLUME I
HENRY POTTER
RALEIGH: PRINTED AND SOLD BY J. GALES, 1821

CHAP. 381.
1793. An act to extend the right of trial by jury to slaves. (Pages 706-707).

1. Be it enacted, &c. That in all cases hereafter happening, where any slave shall be accused of an offence, the punishment whereof shall extend to life, **(See 1816, c. 912, and 1818, c. 972.)** limb, or member, such slave shall be entitled to trial by jury, **(See 1794, c. 412, and 1796, c. 467.)** on oath, consisting of twelve good and lawful men, owners of slaves, in a summary way, and in open court of the county wherein such offence was committed. Provided nevertheless, That if the court of the county shall not meet within fifteen days from the time of commitment, the sherif of the county shall and may summon three justices of the peace of the said county, and a jury of good and lawful men owners of slaves, who shall have as full and ample power and authority to try and

Appendix B
North Carolina Laws

pass sentence on any slave accused and brought to trial before them, as the county court might or could have by virtue of this act. And provided always, That the said jury and three justices shall not be connected with the owner of such slave, or the prosecutor, either by affinity or consanguinity.

2. And be it further enacted, That when a slave shall be apprehended for any offence, the punishment whereof may effect life, member, or limb, it shall be the duty of the sheriff, and he is hereby required to serve the owner of such slave, if known, with notice of trial ten days previous thereto (which notice shall be proved to the court) in order that the owner may have an opportunity of defending the said slave; and the costs of the said notice, and all other costs attending the said trial of any slave so apprehended, where the owner or owners shall be known, shall be paid by the said owner or owners, provided the said slave, if a freeman, would be liable to the payment thereof. And in case of refusal to pay the same, process may issue from the clerk of the court to compel payment, in the same manner as for other costs.

3. And be it further enacted, That when the owner of any slave to be tried by virtue of this act, shall not be known, or cannot be discovered or ascertained, or shall reside out of this state, it shall and may be lawful for the court, and they are hereby authorised and required, to appoint counsel to appear for and in behalf of the prisoner, who shall be allowed the same fees as the attorney for the state is allowed for criminal prosecutions. After which they may proceed to trial in the same manner as if the owner had been notified agreeable to the directions of this act, in which case the fees for the counsel, clerk and sheriff, shall be paid by the county in which the court is held in the same manner as other county charges.

****

LAWS OF THE STATE OF NORTH CAROLINA
REVISED, UNDER THE AUTHORITY OF THE GENERAL ASSEMBLY
VOLUME II
HENRY POTTER
RALEIGH: PRINTED AND SOLD BY J. GALES, 1821

Appendix B
North Carolina Laws

CHAP. 467.
1796. An act making compensation to the owners of outlawed and executed slaves, for the counties of Bladen, Halifax, Granville, Cumberland, Perquimans, Beaufort and Pitt. (Pages 828-829). (Extended to other counties. See 1797, c. 480, s. 1.).

    1. Be it enacted, &c. That when a slave shall be tried in any of the counties aforesaid, and shall be found guilty by the jury of any crime, the punishment whereof shall extend to life, the said jury shall fix and ascertain the value of the said slave, and shall give the said valuation in at the time they return their verdict; which said evaluation shall be certified by the chairman of the court and given to the owner of the said slave, who shall be entitled to receive two thirds of such valuation from the sheriff of any of the said counties in which such slave may have been executed.

    2. Be it further enacted, That when any slave shall be legally outlawed in any of the counties within mentioned, the owner of which shall reside in one of the said counties, and the said slave shall be killed in consequence of such outlawry, the value of such slave shall be ascertained by a jury which shall be empannelled at the succeeding court of the county where the said slave was killed, and a certificate of such valuation shall be given by the clerk of the court to the owner of said slave, who shall be entitled to receive two thirds of such valuation from the sheriff of the county wherein the slave was killed.

    3. Be it further enacted, That the jury who shall try and return the valuation of any negro by them convicted and valued, shall previously enquire whether the owner of the said slave did or did not feed, clothe and treat him or her with the humanity consistent with his or her situation, except such slave was the property of orphans or minors, which if not proven to their satisfaction, that the owner or owners of said slave did feed, clothe or treat him or her in manner aforesaid, then and in that case the owner or owners shall not be entitled to the benefit of this act.

    4. And be it further enacted, That the courts of the several counties aforesaid respectively, shall be, and they are hereby authorised and required when necessary, to lay a tax on all black polls, in any of the said counties where the owner or owners of any slaves shall be entitled to receive pay for the same under this act, sufficient to defray the charge of any of the said counties which shall be made by the owner or owners of any slave under this act; and the sheriff of the said counties respectively, shall collect such tax under the same rules and regulations as are

Appendix B
North Carolina Laws

prescribed for the collection of county taxes, and shall pay to the owner or owners of the slave or slaves valued under this act, when collected, two thirds of the valuation, which shall be certified by the chairman of the court where the same was valued; which certificate together with the owner's receipt shall be a sufficient voucher for him in the settlement of his account with the court; and the said sheriff shall account with the court of his county for any surplus money which shall remain in his hands after paying the certificate or certificates, which shall be obtained and paid under this act; which said surplus shall be received by the said court for the purpose of discharging any similar claim that shall be made for the value of any slave under this act. Provided nevertheless, That this act and no part thereof shall have effect or be construed to extend to any county in this state not herein particularly mentioned and expressly named, or to negroes belonging to persons living out of this state.

CHAP. 480.
1797. An act to amend an act passed in the year one thousand seven hundred and ninety-six, entitled, "An act making compensation to the owners of outlawed and executed slaves for the counties of Bladen, Halifax, Granville, Cumberland, Perquimans, Beaufort and Pitt." (Pages 841-842). (See 1796, c. 467, s. 1.).

    1. Be it enacted, &c. That from and after the passing of this act, the force, meaning and intent of an act passed in the year one thousand seven hundred and ninety-six, entitled, "An act making compensation to the owners of outlawed and executed slaves for the counties of Bladen, Halifax, Granville, Cumberland, Perquimans, Beaufort and Pitt," shall be extended to the counties of Warren, Onslow and Chatham, under the same rules, regulations and restrictions in every respect whatsoever, as fully as if they had been mentioned in the said act; and the courts respectively of the counties of Warren, Onslow and Chatham, shall take notice and be bound by the same accordingly; any thing to the contrary notwithstanding.

CHAP. 719.
1807. An act to amend the penal laws, so far as respects the trial of slaves charged with capital offences. (Page 1113).

    1. Be it enacted, &c. That from and after the passing of this act, all slaves charged with criminal offences, the punishment of which is capital, shall be tried at the regular terms of the county courts **(By**

Appendix B
North Carolina Laws

superior court. See 1816, c. 912.) of the county in which such offences are alleged to have been committed, and under the same rules, regulations and restrictions as by law now directed.

2. Be it further enacted, That so much of the laws now in force as authorises courts to be specially convened for the trial of slaves charged with capital offences, be, and the same is hereby repealed and made void. (See 1793, c. 381.).

CHAP. 912.
1816. An act to amend the laws (See 1741, c. 35, 1793, c. 381, 1807, c.719.) in force respecting the trial of slaves in capital cases. (Page 1354).

1. Be it enacted, &c. That in all cases in which a slave or slaves shall be charged with the commission of an offence, the punishment whereof may extend to life, the superior courts of law shall have exclusive jurisdiction within their respective counties, the trial shall be conducted in the same manner, and under the same rules, regulations and restrictions, as trials of freemen for a like offence are now conducted, except as is hereinafter provided, and notice of trial shall be given to the owner or owners of such slave or slaves, in the manner now directed in the case of the trial of slaves in the county courts.

2. Be it further enacted, That such cases may be removed for trial to an adjoining county, upon affidavit from the owner, or in his absence, of the counsel of such slave or slaves, in the same manner as causes may now be removed by freemen.

3. Be it further enacted, That a slave shall not be tried for a capital offence, but on presentment or indictment of the grand jury, and on his trial shall be entitled to the right of challenge for cause only, which challenge he shall make by and with the advice and assistance of his owner, or in his absence, of his counsel.

4. Be it further enacted, That a slave convicted of a clergiable offence, shall be entitled to the benefit of clergy, in like manner with a free man.

5. Be it further enacted, That in all cases of conspiracy, insurrection, or rebellion of slaves, upon the information, and at the request of any five justices of the peace of the county in which such conspiracy, insurrection, or rebellion shall happen, it shall be the duty of the governor for the time being, to issue a commission of oyer and

Appendix B
North Carolina Laws

terminer, to any of the judges of the superior courts of law, for the trial of such slaves, in the manner prescribed in the act of 1777, chapter 2, (C. 115.) and of 1779, chapter 6. (C. 157.).

6. Be it further enacted, That all laws and clauses of laws, which come within the meaning and purview of this act, be and the same are hereby repealed.

****

THE LAWS OF THE STATE OF NORTH CAROLINA
ENACTED IN THE YEAR, 1820
RALEIGH:PRINTED BY THOMAS HENDERSON JR. PRINTER TO THE STATE 1821

CHAPTER 39
1820. An Act to provide for the payment of costs when a Slave is convicted of a Capital Crime. (Page 38).

1. Be it enacted by the General Assembly of the State of North Carolina, and it is hereby enacted by the authority of the same, That hereafter, when any slave shall be convicted of a capital crime, and executed in consequence of such conviction, the costs of prosecution shall be paid by the county in which such prosecution shall have commenced.
Read three times and ratified in General Assembly,
the 25th day of December, A.D. 1820
R.M. Sanders,
S.H.C.
B. Yancey S.S.
A true Copy   W.M. Hill, Sec'y.

****

THE LAWS OF NORTH CAROLINA
ENACTED IN THE YEAR 1822
RALEIGH: PRINTED BY BELL & LAWRENCE 1823

CHAPTER II.
1822. An act to amend an act, passed in 1821, entitled "an act to promote the administration of justice." (Page 8).

Appendix B
North Carolina Laws

Be it enacted by the General Assembly of the State of North Carolina, and it is hereby enacted by the authority of the same, That when any application shall be made to remove any cause, whether civil or criminal, to an adjacent county for trial, which cause shall have been before removed, it shall be the duty of the person so applying, to set forth, on affidavit, particularly and in detail, the grounds of such application; and the presiding judge may, in his discretion, remove the same to any adjacent county for trial: Provided, That no cause, under any circumstances, shall be removed more than twice.

II. And be it further enacted, That hereafter, on the trial of any slave or slaves for capital offences, if it shall appear to the presiding judge, by affidavit or otherwise, that such slave or slaves cannot have a fair trial in the county wherein the offence is charged to have been committed, it shall, and may be lawful for such judge to order the removal of such cause to an adjacent county for trial, notwithstanding the master or owner of such slave or slaves may neglect or refuse to make an application to the court for that purpose.

****

ACTS PASSED BY THE GENERAL ASSEMBLY OF THE STATE OF NORTH CAROLINA AT ITS SESSION COMMENCING ON THE THE 17TH OF NOVEMBER, 1823 RALEIGH: PRINTED BY J. GALES & SON - STATE PRINTERS. 1824

CHAPTER LI.
1823. An Act declaring the punishment of persons of colour, in certain cases. (Page 42).
Be it enacted by the General Assembly of the State of North Carolina, and it is hereby enacted by the authority of the same, That any person of colour, convicted by due course of law, of an assault with intent to commit rape upon the body of a white female, shall suffer death without the benefit of clergy.

****

ACTS PASSED BY THE GENERAL ASSEMBLY

Appendix B
North Carolina Laws

OF THE STATE OF NORTH CAROLINA AT ITS SESSION COMMENCING ON THE 21ST OF NOVEMBER 1825
RALEIGH: PRINTED BY BELL & LAWRENCE, PRINTERS TO THE STATE, 1826.

CHAPTER XXIV.
1825. An act to amend an act, passed in the year one thousand eight hundred and sixteen, entitled "an act to amend the laws in force respecting the trial of Slaves in capital cases," and to extend the provisions thereof to the trial of Slaves in certain other cases. (Pages 14-15).

Be it enacted by the General Assembly of the State of North Carolina, and it is hereby enacted by the authority of the same, That the Superior Courts of Law within the several counties of this State, shall hereafter have original exclusive jurisdiction of all felonies within clergy, when committed, or alleged to have been committed by any slave or slaves, and the trial of such slave or slaves shall be conducted and prosecuted under the same rules, regulations and restrictions as the trial of a free man, when charged with a like offence: Provided, That when any slave shall be convicted of any clergiable felony, and shall pray for and obtain the benefits of the fourth section of the before mentioned act, the Court shall have power to direct and adjudge such corporal punishment short of death or dismemberment as to the Court shall seem right, under all the circumstances of the case; and the entry of such judgment shall have the same legal effects and consequences, as if the slave or slaves were burned in the hand, as in case of a free man convicted of a similar offence.

****

ACTS PASSED BY THE GENERAL ASSEMBLY OF THE STATE OF NORTH CAROLINA AT THE SESSION OF 1831-1832
RALEIGH: PRINTED BY LAWRENCE & LEMAY PRINTERS TO THE STATE. 1832

Chapter XXX.

Appendix B
North Carolina Laws

1831-1832. An act to amend the fifth section of an act, passed in the year of our Lord one thousand eight hundred and sixteen, chapter nine hundred and twelve, entitled an act for the more speedy trial of slaves in capital cases. (Pages 25-26).

Be it enacted by the General Assembly of the State of North Carolina, and it is hereby enacted by the authority of the same, That in all cases of insurrection or rebellion, or of conspiracy to make insurrection or to murder or rebel or any such contemplated conspiracy, insurrection or rebellion, of any slave or slaves, upon the information and at the request of any five justices of the peace of the county in which conspiracy, insurrection or rebellion shall happen or may be contemplated, the Governor for the time being shall be authorised and have power to issue a commission of Oyer and Terminer to any one of the judges of the Superior Courts of Law; and in case the said judges are necessarily engaged on their circuits, the Governor shall be authorised and have power to issue a commission to one of the judges of the Supreme Court, whose duty it shall be to hold said court forthwith, and shall be clothed with all the powers necessary for the trial of all such slave or slaves that may be charged with any of the before mentioned offences.

II. And be it further enacted, That every judge holding a court of Oyer and Terminer, and the prosecuting officer in behalf of the State attending the said court, shall be entitled to receive the same compensation as may be allowed by the law generally for holding and attending a term of a Superior Court.

III. Be it further enacted, That the prisoner or prisoners who shall be tried before any court of Oyer and Terminer in this State, shall have the right of appeal to the Supreme Court under the rules and regulations now prescribed by law for appeals.

IV. Be it further enacted, That when the prisoner who shall be indicted before a court of Oyer and Terminer in this State, shall, upon upon affidavit of himself or any other person, shew such circumstances and facts to the court as would induce the judge in the regular courts of this State to remove the trial of said indictment out the county, the judge holding such court of Oyer and terminer may in his discretion continue the said indictment and commit or bind over the prisoner as the case may require for trial at the next Superior Court for said county, when the same shall be disposed of according to the rules and regulations in force for the trial of such offences.

Appendix B
North Carolina Laws

V. Be it further enacted, That in all trials of slaves hereafter for capital offences, the defendant Shall be entitled to be tried by a jury composed of the owners of slaves.

Index

Index

[

[?]elton
  Wm., 65

A

Abet
  David, 83
Adams
  Charles, 83
  james, 101
  James, 100, 101, 102
  John, 118
Africa, 80
  Cargo of slaves, 81
  Coast of, 80
Albertson
  B., 67
  Benjamin, 54
  Elias, 66
  Joshua, 67
Alderson
  John, 90
  Mr., 90
Alen
  David, 31
Alexander
  Adam, 83
  Chas., 83
  Evan, 83
  Geo., 83
  Isaac, 83
  W., 83
Allen
  Ally, 61
  Drury, 31
Allin
  William, 31
Allison
  Allison, 116
Allston
  Mr Peter, 139
Alston
  Ann, 76
  Anne, 77
  Peter, 139
  William, 77
  Winifred, 53
  Wm., 76
American Army
  Establishment of, 155
Ancrum
  John, 127
Anderson
  Lewis, 28
Arkill
  William, 106
  Wm., 106
Armisted
  Anthony, 58, 59
Armstrong
  Capt., 153, 154
Arnold
  Benjamin, 67
Ash
  John B., 145
  Sam, 37
  Saml., 35
Ashbury
  Joseph, 136
Ashe
  John B., 70
  John B., CS, 70
  John B., SC, 64, 65, 69
  Sam, SS, 38
  Saml., 38
Atchison
  William, 112, 113
Averett
  Arthur, 141
Averitt
  Arthur, 140

B

Badget
  Jno, 28
Bagly
  Nathan, 67
Bailey
  John, 66
Baird

Index

Alexr., 143, 144, 149
Benj., 143, 144
Baker
  John, Sheriff, 14
  Saml., 103
Baldwin
  Daniel, 67
  James, 103, 104
  Jesse, 67
  Mr. James, 104
  Wm., 67
Bangs
  Jonathan, 97
Barker
  Mr. Thomas, 2
  T., 150
  Thomas, 149
Barrow
  J:, 101
  John, 100, 101, 102, 105, 134
  Mr. Richard, 101
  Mr. Richd., 102
  Richard, 101, 102
  Richd., 100
  T, 105, 134
Bartram
  William, 103
  Willm., 103
  Wm., 107
  Wm:, 104
Bass
  Benjamin, 28
  Edward, 28
  Rubin, 28
Baucum
  Nicholas, 97
  Sarah, 97
Baver
  Daniel, 83
Beals
  John, Jr., 66
Beard
  Richard, 66
  William, 66
Bearden
  Ben, 28
  Benjamin, 31
Beasley
  John, 142
Beasly
  John, 143
Becton
  Frederick, 136
  Fredk., 136
Beeson
  Richard, 66
Belk
  Darling, 83
  James, 83
Bell
  Archd., 133
  Archibald, 132
  Geo., 30
  Lewis, 17
  Richard, 106
Benboe
  Benja., 67
Benbury
  John, 131
  M, 32
  Samuel, 114, 118
  Samuell, 113
  Tho., SC, 56
  Thomas, 41, 149
  Thomas, Esqr., 50
  Thos, 40
  Thos., 34, 39, 40, 41, 44, 47, 150
  Thos., SC, 39, 47
  Thos:, 132
Bennett
  Bennett, 149
  William, 142, 143
  Willm., 150
Benning
  Arthur, Sheriff, 11
Benton
  JS, 127
Berhan
  Danl., 83
Bignall
  Robert, 61
Black
  Ezekiel, 83
  Thomas, 83
  Wm., 83
Blacke
  William, Junr., 83
  William, Senr., 83
Blackledge
  Richard, 24, 136
  Richard, Esqr., 24
  Richd, 25
  Richd., 136
Blackmons
  Mr., 36
Blair
  Geo., 114, 131
  George, 113, 131
Blake
  Thos., 139
Blalok
  Jeams, 83
Blanchard
  Andrew, 32
Blaning
  Mrs. Elizabeth, 127
Blanings

Index

Eliz., 127
Blanning
  Hugh, 104
Blin
  Daniel, 100
  Danl., 101, 102
  Mr. Daniel, 101, 102
Bloodworth
  Mr., 64, 72
  Thomas, 139
Blount
  Charles, 106
  Fred, 118
  Jacob, 25
  Jacob, JP, 24
  James, 69, 70, 71, 142, 143
  James Esqr., 142
  Joseph Esquire, 114
  Mr A., 76
  Mr,, 143
  Mr., 33, 68, 150
  Mr. Charles, 11
  Mr. James, 33
Blue
  Steven, 83
Bodiley
  Joshua, Esqr., 9
Bond
  Edward, 66
  Hance, 151
  Job, 65
  Mr. James, 131
Bondfield
  Mr. Charles, 114
Bonds
  Mr., 64
Bonfield
  Charles, Keeper of the Goal, 23

Bonner
  Elizabeth, 17, 114
  Henry, 17, 113, 114
  Tho, 134
  Thomas, 113, 134
  Thos, 135
  Thos., 114
Borden
  William, 44, 45
Boswell
  Ransom, 31
Bould
  George, 97
  Gorge, 97
Boyd
  R, 105
  R., 101, 102
  Robert, 100, 101, 102
  Robert Esqr., 101
  Robt., 105
  William, 142, 143
  Wm., 129
Brack
  Geo., 130
Bradby
  Richard, 127
Bradley
  JW, 147
Bragg
  John, 30
Brandon
  Jno, 116
  Richd., 116
Branson
  Thomas, 66
Brattain
  Robert, 66
Brevard

John Esqr., 116
  Robt., 116
Brewster
  L.H., 50
Brickell
  Math., 115
Bridges
  Lockwoods folly, 138
Brin
  John, 140
Brinion
  John, 141
British Enemy
  Destruction of property, 44
  Incursion of, 44
British Troops, 57
Brothers
  Samuel, 66
Brown
  Geo., 140
  James, 66
  Jno, JP, 58
  Jno., 147
  John, 107, 115, 123, 124
  Michael, 116
  Thos, 57
  Thos., 139
  Thos., JP, 58
  William, 134
  Willm., 135
  Wm., 134, 135
Brownrigg
  Geo., 118
  George, 113, 114, 118
  Richard, 129
  Richard Esqr., 128, 129
  Richd. Esqr., 129

Index

Bryan
  John, 32, 97, 98
  Mr., 44
  Nathan, 32
  Simon, 96
  Symon, 95
  Thomas, 103, 107
  Thos., 104
  William, 32, 50, 51
  william, Esqr., 44
  William, Esquire, 43
  Wm., 50, 51
Buck
  Capt., Estate of, 13
Buckhanan
  Wm., 31
Bundy
  Caleb, 67
  Demsey, 67
  Joseph, 66
  Josiah, 66
  Samuel, 66
Bunker
  Reuben, 67
Burgess
  Lovatt, 148
Burgwin
  J., Clerk, 26
  John, 120, 121, 125
Burgwine
  John, 119
Burk
  Chas., 25
Burke
  Thom, 83
Burny
  John, 1
Burton
  Richd, 28
Butler
  Thomas, 28
Byars
  William, 31

C

Cabarrus
  M., 146
  Mr., 70, 146, 150
Cain
  John, Esqr., 79
Caita
  Mr., 100
Calvert
  Maxl., 112
  Maxmilian, 112
Cambell
  Alexander, 83
Campbell
  Alexander, 35
  Alexr., 35
  Danl., 58
  George, 20, 118
  James, 111
  Jas., 111
  John, 119, 120, 121, 122, 123
  Mr., 68, 125
  William, 119, 120
  William Esqr., 125
  William, Esqr., 22
  Wm., 120
Camps
  Moors Creek, 158
Cane
  Willm., 103
Cannady
  Charles, 67
Cannan
  Jacob, 66
Cannon
  William, 17
Carns
  Alxr., 83
  Daniel, 83
Carruthers
  Jos, Sheriff, 6
  Joseph, Sheriff, 4
Carson
  Jas, 116
Carter
  Isaac, 115
Cary
  Colo. Wilson, 23
Caryl
  Joseph, 83
Cason
  Thomas, 83
Caswell
  Governor, 158
  R., SP, 50, 56
  R., Sp., 52
  R., Speaker, 27
  Rd., 159
  Richd. Esqr., 159
  Wm., 159
Caudill
  Isom, 28
  James, 28
Cawthon
  William, 28
Chambers
  John, 31
Chamness
  William, 66
Chapman
  Isabel, 87
Chaponel, 88
  Monsieur, 89

Index

Charly
  Charly, 66
Chatham County
  Iron Works, 34
Chatham County
  Iron WorksIron
  Works, 31
Chavis
  Gibea, 28
  William, 28
Cheek
  William, 123
  Wm, 124
Cherry
  John, 14
  Lamuel, 105
Chery
  Leml, 105
Chiles
  Nathan, 28, 31
Chisson
  Mr., 90
Clapp
  John Philip, 42, 43
  Philip, 42
Clark
  Benjamin, 39, 139
  Mr Benjamin, 39
  Mr. Benjamin, 39
Clayton
  Francis, 127
  Mr. Fras., 126
Clear
  Timo., 136
  Timothy, 136
Clegg
  Samuel, 63
Clifton
  Ezekl:, 145
Clinton

Richd., 132, 133
Clitherall
  John, 24
Cochran
  John, 83
  Thomas, 83
Cock
  Winifred, 53
Cocke
  Joseph, 53
  Winifred, 53
Coffin
  Aaron, 66
  Abijah, 67
  Barnabas, 66
  Benjamin, 66
  Matthew, 65
  William, Junr., 67
  Wm., 67
Cogdell
  R., 25
  Richard, 24, 136
  Richard, Esqr., 24
  Richd., 136
Collins
  Lewis, 28
  Thomas, 58, 59
Coltrane
  David, 2
Committee of
  Claims Reports, 94
Conegie
  George, 104
Connor
  Ja., 83
Conway
  Peter, Clerk, 4
  Peter, Clerk of Court, 6
Cook

Abram, 67
Isaac, 83
Thomas, 16, 66, 124
Thos., 124
Cooke
  Jno., 138
  John, Attorney, 33
  Mr, 33
Coor
  James, 135
  James, SS, 70
  jams., SS, 64
  Jams., SS, 65
Coors
  Jams., SS, 69
Corbin
  Doctr. John, 122
  Edmund, 73
  Francis, 74
  Francis, Esqr., 19
  Jean, 72, 74
  Jean, Will of, 73
Corbyn
  Doctor, 11
  Doctor John, 121
Corprew
  Joshua, 112
  Mr. Thomas, Estate of, 11
Cosen
  Gabriel, 67
Cotanche
  Captn. Michl., 100, 101, 102
  Michel, 101
Courts
  District Halifax Superior Court, 94

Index

Magistrates and
  Freeholders
  Courts, 93
New Bern
  District
  Superior Court,
  94
Cowan
  Capt., 160
Cox
  Moses Junr., 130
Craig
  Moses, 83
  Thomas, 26
Crawford
  John, 12
Cray
  William, 15, 18,
    71, 140
  Willm., 141
  Wm., 130, 141
  Wm. junr., 142
Creecy
  Mr., 71
Creeks
  Core Creek, 43
  Moor's, 157
Crews
  Hardy, 31
Crimes
  Assisted Murder,
    135
  Attempted
    Murder, 107,
    114, 116
  Breaking &
    Entering, 101,
    102, 108, 135
  Burglary, 95, 135
  Burglary &
    Felony, 110

Disobedience of
  Orders, 153
Felony, 95, 99,
  112, 143, 145,
  149
Felony Poisoning,
  124, 127, 130,
  151
Felony Theft, 105
Intent to Poison,
  142
Jail Breaking,
  100
Murder, 103,
  118, 122, 131,
  134, 138, 146,
  147
Rape, 97, 113,
  132, 140
Robbery, 98, 119,
  120, 121, 127
Runaway, 125
Stealing, 140
Theft, 102
Trading with
  Slaves, 138
Crow
  Samuel, 83
Cry
  James, 83
Crye
  John, 83, 84
Cunningham
  Thomas, 108, 110
  Thos., 108
Curry
  Genl. Ben, 49
Custis
  Hancock, 134
  Handcock, 134

D

Dalrymple
  Mr. John, 6
Danbibin
  Da[?], 108
Daniel
  John, 12
Davenport
  Frances, 28
Davis
  Adam, 83
  Gao[?], 145
  Good., 151
  Humphry, 28
  Isral, 83
  James, JP, 6
  James:, 83
  Jas., 4
  Jesse, 66
  John, 28, 83
  Joshua, 65
Davisons
  George, 116
Dawson
  Levi, 136
De Rosset, 111
  Armand, 111
  Lewis Henry,
    Esqr., 15
Deadman
  Doctor Jacob, 16
Delon
  Mark, 66
Dennis
  John, 31
Derosset
  Armand, 111
Deter
  James, 83
Dickins
  R., 71

206

Index

R., CM, 72
Dicks
  Joshua, 67
Dillon
  Peter, 67
Dixon
  Major, 158
Dolvin
  John, 61
Dotey
  Benajah, 130, 141
Doty
  Benajah, 140
Downey
  James, 28, 55
  Robert, 28, 31
Downing
  John, 83
Dry
  Mr., Sheriff, 7
Du Bois
  Captn., 109
  Jno., 109
  John, 109
DuBois
  Capt. John, 3
  Jno., 110
  John, 140
  John Esqr., 109, 119
Duboise
  John Esqr., 108
  John, Esqr., 11
  John, Executors of, 21
Dudley
  William, 99
Dukins
  Robert, CS, 70
Dunbiben
  Jonathan, 139

Dunbibin
  Danl., 110, 111
Dunbibins
  Danl, 111
Duncomb
  Mr. Samuel, 16
Dupre
  Sarah, 86
Dupre'
  Mr. Lewis, 87
  Sarah, 87
Dupree
  Mrs, 138
  Mrs., 40
  Mrs. Sarah, 40, 84
  Sarah, 40, 79
Duprees
  Mrs., 139
Duty
  Richard, 31
Dwight
  Mr Samuel, 138
  Mr Samuell, 138

E

Earle
  Daniel, 118
Eaton
  Col. William, 46
  Coll. William, 3
  Colo. William, 60
  Mr., 61
  William, 46
  William, Esqr., 47
  William, Esquire, 60
Edmonds
  Howell, Sheriff, 21

Edwards
  Thomas, 18
Elbeck
  Montfort, 145
Ellegood
  Mathias, 129
Elliot
  Jacob, 66
Ellis
  Evan, 107
Ellison
  Axom, 66
Elmore
  Areelous, 66
  Thos., 66
England
  Liverpoole, 118
Enoch
  Robert, 83
Etord[?]
  Will, 138, 139
Eugan
  Darby, 7
Evans
  Bartholomew, 95, 96
  John, 140
  William, 127
Evens
  Jesse, 67

F

Fagans
  George, 28
Fallaw
  Elizabeth, 113
Faries
  Isaac, 109
Farlow
  Nathan, 66
Farmer

Index

Josiah, 31
Fauquier
  Fran:, 113
  Francis Esq, 112
Ferril
  Micajah, 67
Finley
  Charles:, 83
  James, 83
  William, 84
Fishear
  Pall, 83
  William, 83
Fisher
  Charles, 83
  Frederick, 83
Fitt
  Thomas, 79, 80, 81
  Thos., 80
Flemming
  Elizabeth, 19
Fontaine
  Elizabeth, 5
Fontaines
  Elizabeth, 5
  Jno., 5
Forbas
  Hugh, 84
Forest
  John, 84
Fort
  Elias, 61
Franklin
  Mr., 64
Franklyn
  Bently, Deputy Sheriff, 13
Frazier
  Sam, 136
  Samuel, 136
Free Negroes & Mulatoes, 27
  Petition of, 27
Free Negroes and Slaves
  Insolent behaviour of, 29
Freeman
  Michael, 83
Frohock
  Mr. John, 8
Fromigg
  Aaron, 66
Fulford
  Mr Joseph, 28

G

Galespee
  Mr., 72
Galt
  Hugh, 31
Gardner
  Isaac, 67
  Mr., 64
  William, 66
Gaskins
  Adam, 30
Gaston
  Alexander, 32, 33
  Alxr., 25
  Doctr., 24
  Mr, 33
  Mr., 33
Gates
  Lovet, 28, 31
gaylord
  Benj., 137
  Benjamin, 137
Geckie
  Jas., 86
Geddy
  Jno, 151
Gee
  Hancle[?], 145
  Howell, 148
Gekie
  James, 85
  Corneige, 102
George
  David, 95, 96
  James, 95, 96
Georgia Towns
  Savannah, 69
Germain
  Robert, 145
Gibbens
  John, 83
Gibbs
  George, 146
  George Esqr., 146
  Robert, 37, 38
  William, 37, 38
Giddy
  John, 63
  John, Sheriff, 63
Gifford
  Isaac, 129
  Jonathan, 66
Gilbert
  Jeremiah, 67
Gilespie
  John, 83
Gilliam
  Mr. Hinchia, 78
Gillispie
  Mr., 90
Gilmour
  William, 151
Glover
  William, 31
Godfrey

Index

Matthew, 112, 113
Gold
  Sarah, 63, 147, 148
Good
  William, 136
  Wm., 136
Gordon
  John, 83
  Joshua, 83
Governor Martin, 45
Grag
  Frederick, 108
Gragg
  Fredk., 108
  William, 31
Graham
  Geo, 83
  Mr. Richard, 5
Grahon
  John, 83
Grainger
  Jos, 108
  Joshua, 108
Granger
  Jas, CS, 38
  Jas., 37
  Jas., CS, 38
Grant
  Alexander, 15, 16
  Reuben, 71
Graves
  Elijah, 55, 56
  Henry, 31
  Mr. Thomas, 4
  Thos., 6
Gray
  Alexander, 83
  Gray, 150
  Jacob, 83

Mr. William, 58, 59
  Sampson, 83
  Shared, 83
Great Britain, 35, 36
Green
  Jams., Senr., 5
  John, 46, 47, 60, 142, 143
  John Senr., 103
  Matthew, 141
  Mr., 61
  Mr. John, 60
Greers
  John, 83
Gregg
  Frederick, 119, 120, 122, 127
  Fredk., 110, 123
Gregory
  Isaac, 129
  James, 96, 110
  Mr. James, 96
Grenada
  Negroes imported from, 36
Grifee
  John, 83
Griffin
  Amaus, 66
Grimes
  Robert, 144
Grise
  Richd., 105
Guinn
  Nathaniel, 137
Guion
  Mr., 90
Gwin
  John, 28

H

Hair
  Richd., 100
Hall
  Doctor Thomas, 127
  Doctr. Thos., 127
  Mrs., 128
  Mrs. Lucy, 128
  Simon, 30
  Thomas, 83
  Thos., 128
Halsey
  Halsey, 118
  J., 106
  Jer., 118
  John, 106
  William, Sheriff, 9
Hamm
  Philip, 66
Hammond
  John, 11
Hancocke
  Nat, 130
Hanson
  Erasmus, 139
Hardy
  Robert, 113, 115
  Robt, 115
  Robt., 114
Hare
  John, 115
Harell
  James Junr., 121
  James Junr. Esqr., 120
Haren
  John, 115
Harget
  Mr., 64

Index

Hargroe
  John, 46, 59
Hargrove
  John, 60
Harlan
  Enoch, 66
Harmon
  Henry, 8
Harnet
  Cornelius, 120
  Cornelius Esqr., 108
Harnett
  Cornelious, 109
  Cornelius, 36, 111, 119, 121, 125
  Cornelius, Esqr., 8
  Cornl., 109, 110, 111
  Cornls., 108, 119
  Corns., 120
Harper
  Ambrose, 148
Harrell
  Saml., Clerk of Court, 62
Harrington
  Genl., 41
  Henry William, 41
Harris
  John, 28
  Richd., 31
Hart
  Anthony, 151
  Benjamin, Coroner, 11
  Henry Philip, 31
  John, 28
Harvey
  Jesse, 66
  Thomas, 77, 78
Hasell
  James, Esqr., 21
  James, Junr., Esqr., 22
Hatch
  Lemuel, 145
Haughton
  Jeremiah, 142, 143
Hawkins
  Philemon, 123, 124
Haworth
  [Torn], 66
Haywood
  J, Cs, 76
  J, CS, 50, 52, 55, 68, 79, 81, 85, 90
  J., 82, 146, 147, 150
  J. Haywood, CS, 50
  J., Clk, 65
  J., Cs, 69
  J., CS, 56, 61, 64, 70, 72, 76, 77, 86
  Jno., CS, 43
Head
  Isaac, 28
  John, 28
  Richd., 31
  Thomas, 28, 31
  William, 28
Hedge Beth
  Carter, 28
Helms
  Jeremiah, 148
Henby
  John, 66
  Joseph, 67
  William, 66
Henderson
  Nathaniel, 123
  Nathl, 124
Hendrick
  Benjamin, 28
Henley
  Joseph, 54
Hewes
  Joseph, 131, 142, 143
Hiatt
  Asher, 67
  Christr., Junr., 67
  Jona., 67
  Solomon, 67
Hicks
  Benjamin, 63
High
  Capt., 159
Hight
  Alsey, 159
  Capt., 159
Hill
  Aaron, Junr., 66
  Elizabeth Henry, 53
  Henry, 53, 79, 80, 115
  Joseph, 28, 66
  Martha, 19, 23, 26
  Thomas, 53, 66
  Thomas T., 53
  Wm., 66
Hinson
  David, 83
Hix
  Benj., 143
  Benjamin, 149

Index

Capt., 149
Hodge
  Alexr., 83
Hodges
  Thomas, 61
Hodgson
  George, 67
  Jno., 118
  John, 66, 118
  Joseph, 66
  Robert, 66
  Thomas, 66
Hogan
  Colo., 159
Hoggat
  [Torn], 66
  Aaron, 66
  Jesse, 65
  Joseph, 65
  Moses, 66
  Stephanas, 66
  William, 66
Hoggatt
  John, 65
Holders
  F., 147
Hollowell
  Thos, 66
Holmes
  Gabriel, 132, 133
Hooper
  Mr., 72
Horniblow
  John, 142, 143
Hoskins
  William, 106
  Wm., 2, 3
Houston
  James, 83
How
  Job, Sheriff, 7
Howard

Groves, 28
  James, 130, 140
  James Esqr., 140
  Jas., 141
  John, 99
  Martin Esqr., 126
Howcalt
  Edward, 100
  Mr., 100
Howe
  Mr, 27
  Robert, Esqr., 27
  Robert, Esquire, 27
Howell
  John, 66
Howes
  Job, 98, 99
Howey
  George, 83
  John, 83
Hoyle
  James, 99
Huces
  John, 1
Huckaby
  Samuel, 28
Hudjons
  Cutbird, 28
Huffham
  Hudlin, 122
Hughes
  Charles, 58
Hughs
  Chas., 59
Hughy
  John, 83
Hunt
  Abner, 67
  Asa, 67
  Eleazer, 67
  Isaiah, 67

J, 41, 47, 49, 68, 150
J, CHC, 41, 47, 55, 77, 80, 81, 85, 86, 90
J, Clk, 68, 76
J., 44, 143, 146, 147
J., CHC, 56, 70
J., Clk, 64, 65, 71, 72, 74, 76
Jacob, 67
Jno., 158
John, 35, 39, 40
John, CHC, 34, 37, 38, 39
John, Clerk of House of Commons, 32
M., 49
Memucan, 55
Nathan, 67
William, 67
Wm., 67
Hunter
  Thomas, 95
  Thos., 96
Hurst
  James, 113, 114
Hussey
  Tho., 67
Hutchings
  John, 112
  Joseph, 112
Hutchison
  Wm., 83

I

Iddings
  Benjamin, 66
  Joseph, 66

Index

Indians
  Indian Boy taken prisoner from Cherokee Nation, 35
  Indian Scalps, 8
  Indian Slavery, 35
  Mistreatment of an Indian servant, 32
  War against, 28
  War between 1709 & 1719, 28
Ingram
  John, JP, 74
Ivey
  William, 112

J

Jack
  Capt., 154, 162
Jackson
  Thomas, 46, 59, 60
  Wm., 151
Jacocks
  Jona., Sheriff, 58
Jamaica, 36
  Negroes from, 36
Jarmain
  Robert, 144
Jarman
  Rob, 97
  Robert, 97
  Robt., 52
Jenings
  Jno., 144, 149
  Thos., 144, 149
Jennings
  John, 143
  Thomas, 144
Jermain
  Robert, 52
Jesop
  Caleb, 67
Jeter
  James, 12
  James:, 12
  Saml., 31
Johnson
  Abraham, 59, 60
  Benja., 67
  Caleb, 67
  Isham, 28
  James, 67
  Joshua, 65
  M. Duke, Clk, 76
  Robert, 66
  Will, JP, 26
  William, 123
  Willm., 124
Johnston
  Abraham, 46
  Henry, 72
  Mr., 90
  Thomas Esqr., 140
  Thomas, Sheriff, 79
  Thos., 130
  Thos., Sheriff, 141
Jones
  Abijah, 66
  Allen, 158
  Allen, SS, 39, 40
  Edward, 123, 124
  Frederick, 125
  Griffeth, 107
  Griffith, 103
  Isaac, 66, 107
  Jno., 107
  John, 145
  Miss, 49, 50
  Miss Ann, 50
  Miss Nancy, 49, 50
  Mr., 118
  Mr.Thos., 11
  Thomas, 10
  Thomas, Clerk of Court, 23
  William, 125
  Willie, 21
Jordain
  Isaac, 58
  Mr., 58
Jordan
  Charles, 24
  Jonah, 66
  Richd, 67
  Thomas, 66
Joyner
  Bridgiman, 145
  Henry, 145
Justice
  John, 59, 60
Justiss
  John, 46

K

Kenan
  James, 132, 133
  James, Sheriff, 17
  Owen, 132, 133
Kersey
  Amos, 66
  Daniel, 66
  Jesse, 65
  Thomas, 65
Kibble
  Jas., 130
Kinchen

Index

John, 151
Kindred
  John, 62
Kindreds
  John, 62
King
  John, 83
  Solomon, 105, 106
Kirkpatrick
  Wm., 147
Knight
  Ephraim, 88, 90
  Epm., 89
  Jonathan, 31, 55
  Martha, 28
  William, 31
Knox
  Mr. Andrew, Sheriff, 9
Kornegue
  George, 103

L

Lamb
  Phineas, 65
  Restone, 65
  Robert, 66
  Simeon, 67
  Zachariah, 65
Lancaster
  Mr. Sanders, 74
  William, 75
  William Sanders, 74, 75
  Wm. Sanders, 75
Lane
  JS, 2
  Mr., 97
  Walter, 97
Lanier
  Burwell, 132, 133
  William, 105
  Wm, 105
Lathan
  John, 83
Laurence
  Jno., 65
Lawson
  Moses, 83
Lee
  Bryant, 122
  Mary, 122
  Mr. Stephen, 99
  Steven, 99
Leech
  Jos., 4
  Jos., JP, 5
Legatt
  Will, 83
Legget
  John, 41
  John, gone over to the enemy, 41
Leigh
  Gilbert, 131, 132, 150
LeKey
  Robert, 83
  Thos., 83
Lesley
  James, 83
Lewis
  Howell, 55
  Richard, 2
Lindsay
  John, 62
Lindsey
  John, 151
Lock
  Colo., 160
  Francis, Sheriff, 19
  Joseph, 56
  Mr Joseph, 57
Locke
  Joseph, 56, 57
Lockey
  Hen:, 135
  Henry, 135
London
  John, 120, 122, 123, 125
Long
  James, Estate of, 9
  L., 151
  Mr, 68
  Nicholas, 145, 147, 151
Lovick
  Thomas, 88, 89
Lowe
  Thos., 28
Lowery
  James, 83
Lowrie
  Anthony, 99
Lucas
  Willm., 58
Lucky
  Robert, 83
Lundy
  Amos, 66
  Richard, 66
Luten
  Thomas, 106
  Thos., 106
  William, 106
  Wilm., 106
Lynch
  George, 61
Lyon
  James, 103
  Jno, 111

Index

John, 108, 111, 119, 120, 121, 122, 123
Lytle
  Lieut Willm., Court Martial of, 153
  Lieut., 153, 154, 158, 162
  Lieut. Willm., 153

M

Macey
  Henry, 66
  Joseph, 66
Mackenzie
  C., 68
  Christian, 68
  William, 68
MacKenzie
  John, 110
  William, 110
Mackey
  John, 83
Macknight
  Thos., 129
Maclaine
  Archibald, 73
  M, 32
Macon
  John, 3
Macy
  David, 67
  John, 67
  Matthew, 66
  Micajah, 67
  Paul, 67
  Tho., 67
  Timothy, 67
Manly

Basil, 58
Marshall
  Saml., 123
  Samuel, 122
Marshill
  Thomas, 66
Martin
  Alex., SS, 42
  Alexr, SS, 81
  JA, 83
  Jo., 30
  Josiah, Governor, 29
  Mr., 76
Mask
  Wm., 143, 144
Mast
  John, 66
  Wm., 149
Matthews
  William, 28
Maultsby
  John, 108, 128
May
  Enoch, 67
McCallum
  James, 31
McCamon
  John, 83
McCane
  Andw., 83
  Hugh, 83
  Hugh, Senr., 83
  John, 83
  William, 83
McCashlan
  James, 83
McClaine
  Mr., 72
McCloys
  Margaret, 5
McClure

Mat, 83
  Richard, 3
McComb
  Saml., 83
McCorkel
  Mrs., 110
McCoy
  Margaret, 5
  Robert, 67
McCrary
  Hugh, 84
McCulloch
  Geo., 139, 140
McCulloh
  Jno, 83
McDowell
  Mr., 72
McElroy
  James, 83
  John, 83
McKay
  Mr., 90
McKenzie
  Christian, 67, 69
McKinzie
  John, 110
McKiskin
  Donald, 107
McKnight
  Mr., 31
  Thomas, Negroes of, 32
McKorkel
  James, 83
  Owen, 83
McKorkrl
  Archd, 83
McLin
  Thomas, 37, 38
McManey
  William, 83
McNeely

Index

John, 83
McNelley
  John, 84
McRee
  Wm., 147
McWhorter
  George, 83
  James, 83
  Moses, 83, 84
Mearns
  William, 106
Meeting House
  fishing Creek, 148
Mendenhall
  [Torn], 66
  Aaron, 67
  Benjamin, 65
  Isaac, 65
  John, 66
  Joseph, 66
  Mordecai, 66
  Mordica, 65
  Moses, 65, 66
  Richard, 66
Menzies
  Frances, 72
Merret
  Thomas, Goaler, 16
Merritt
  Thomas, 117
Metcalf
  George, 67
Migee
  John, 83
Miller
  Abraham, 83
  James, 35
  John, 63, 147, 148
  Mr James, 35

Ralph, 104, 128
Mills
  [Torn], 66
  Amos, 66
  John, 66
Mils
  Benona, 67
Ming
  Thomas, 150
Mins
  Capt., 25
Mircoll
  Davie, 28
Mires
  Harmon, 83
Mitchel
  Col., 71
Mitchell
  Abrm., 99
  Geo., 141
  George, 141
Modlin
  John, 66
Montfort
  M., 146
  Mr., 146
Moor
  Andrew, 83
  David, 83
  James, 83
  Joseph, 83
Moore
  Amye (free negro), 126
  Capt. John, 158
  Charles, 28
  David, 83
  George, Esqr., 3
  James, 132, 133
  Jno, 86
  Jno., JP, 86
  John, Esquire, 85

Joshua, 66
M, 128
Maurice Esqr., 126
Samuel, 66
Thomas, 66
Moorhead
  Jas., 147
Moran
  James, 111
  Jas, 122
More
  Capt. Robt., 158, 159
Morgan
  Charles, 67
  James, 67
  John, 31
Morris
  Aaron, 66
  Hav[?], Junr., 67
  Jno., 111
  John, 110, 111
  Jonathan, 67
  Joseph, 66, 67
  Mordecai, 66
  Nathan, 67
  Thomas, 66
Mortimore
  Mr John, 7
Munden
  Levi, 54
Murray
  John, 73
  John, Esqr., 73

N

Nash
  A, 34
  A., Speaker, 37, 38

Index

Abner, 137
Nassery
   Wm., 117
Nc Counties
   Beaufort, 45
   Cumberland, 36
NC Counties
   Anson, 12
   Beaufort, 20
   Bertie, 2, 15, 19, 23, 26, 58
   Bladen, 22, 39, 41, 56
   Brunswick, 40, 84, 87
   Bute, 16, 24
   Carteret, 44
   Chatham, 31, 77
   Chowan, 16, 19, 23, 50
   Craven, 4, 8, 9, 33, 43, 51, 88
   Dobbs, 18
   Duplin, 7, 9, 17
   Edgecombe, 16
   Edgecombe, 11, 62
   Granville, 3, 27, 30, 55
   Greene, 64
   Guilford, 42, 43
   Halifax, 13, 20, 46, 47, 59, 60, 63, 88, 90
   Hertford, 13, 62
   Hyde, 90
   Johnston, 84
   Jones, 52
   Mecklenburg, 82
   New Hanover, 3, 10, 11, 12, 15, 21, 72, 85

Northampton, 20, 21, 60
Onslow, 12, 15, 18, 71, 79
Pasquotank, 2, 10
Perquimans, 78
Pitt, 13
Rowan, 19, 43
Sullivan, 64
Wake, 42
Warren, 77
Washington, 64
Wayne, 74
Nc County
   Wake, 159
NC County
   Beaufort, 101, 105, 126, 133, 134
   Bladen, 102, 103, 104, 107, 128, 139, 146
   Brunswick, 138, 139, 155
   Bute, 123
   Caswell, 158
   Chatham, 158
   Chowan, 105, 113, 117, 128, 131, 132, 142, 143, 149
   Craven, 96, 136, 137
   Duplin, 132, 157
   Edgecombe, 117, 147
   Halifax, 145, 147, 151, 157
   Hertford, 114
   Hyde, 137
   Jones, 145

Montgomery, 143, 149
New Hanover, 98, 108, 109, 110, 120, 121, 122, 123, 125, 155
Onslow, 99, 129, 140, 141
Pasquotank, 95, 128, 129
Rowan, 116, 155, 160
Wake, 159
NC Districts
   Edenton, 154
   Halifax, 154
   Hillsborough, 154, 157
   New Bern, 126
   Newbern, 154
   Salisbury, 154, 157
   Wilmington, 154
NC Towns
   Bath, 29
   Bath Town, 100, 101, 102, 105
   Beaufort, 88
   Edenton, 2, 17, 23, 29, 50, 81, 105, 113, 118, 131, 142
   Elizabeth Town, 147
   Enfield, 148
   Fayette Ville, 89
   Fayetteville, 74, 75, 85, 86, 143
   Halifax, 78, 147, 151
   Hillsborough, 44, 60, 61

Index

New Bern, 4, 5, 52, 96, 126, 135
Newbern, 8, 24, 27, 29, 159
Purisbury, 153
Swannsborough, 71
Tarborough, 24
Tarbro, 61
Wilmington, 10, 35, 39, 57, 68, 110, 119, 120, 121, 122, 123, 125, 126
Windsor, 58, 59, 81
Winton, 62
Nealey
  Chrisr., CC, 43
Nelson
  Alexr., 83
  Jn., 83
Newby
  Exum, 67
  Samuel, 66
  Thos., 67
Newman
  John, 135
  Thomas, 89, 90
Newton
  George, 31
  Wilson, 112
Nicholls
  Humphry, Sheriff, 17
Nichols
  Christopher, 66
  Isaac, 2
  Julius, 25
  Julius, Sheriff, 24, 25

P Julius, 124
Nicholson
  Christopher, Junr., 66
Nixon
  John, 67
  Phineas, 66
  Robert, 140
  Robt., 141
  Zachariah, 67
Norman
  George, 31
Norris
  James, 28
North
  Jas, 83
Northern States, 54
Nunn
  Joshua, 31

O

Oacock Barr, 29
Ocacock Barr, 30
Oliphant
  Wm., 58, 147
Oliver
  John, 8
O'Neill
  Tho., 103
Ormand
  Roger, Sheriff, 14
  Wyriot, 14
Ormond
  Henry, 20, 134
  Henry Esqr., 134, 135
  Mr., 102
  William, 105
  Wyecott Esqr., 134
Orr

James, 83
Robt., 83
Osborn
  Alexr, 83
Overman
  Charles, 67
  Ephraim, 66
  James, 67
  John, 66
  Onidas, 66
  Thomas, 67
Owen
  Mr. Thomas, 34
Owens
  William, 31
Ozburn
  Daniel, 66
  David, 66
  Joseph, 67
  Peter, 67
  Samuel, 66
  William, 67

P

Palin
  Thos, 66
Parfett
  Benjamin, a seaman, 24
Parker
  George, 127
  James, 10
  James, Estate of, 10
  Job, 67
  Nathan, 67
Parkinson
  Jams., 6
  Mr. James, 4
Parks
  Hugh, 83

Index

Parmela
   Benjamin, 37, 38
Pasteur
   Charles, 46, 59, 60
Paton
   A., 49
Patterson
   Robert, 150
Pattison
   Joseph, 66
   William, 66
Pay
   Michl., 150
Payne
   Michl., 81
   Peter, 106
Peacock
   William, 9
Peasley
   Col. John, 42
Peddwick
   Benja., 129
Pendleton
   Thomas, 95
   Thos., 96
Pendry
   James, 65
Perry
   Nicholas, 115
Person
   Genl. Thomas, 34
   Mr., 32
   Thomas, 81
Peterson
   Thomas, 66
Pettiford
   Lawrence, 28
Phillips
   John, 61
   Mr. Ethelred, 62
Pidgeon
   Samuel, 65
Piggatt
   William, 65
Pike
   Nathan, 66
Pilkington
   Captn. Seth, 100, 101
Pilots
   Petition of, 29
Pittard
   Saml., 31
Player
   William, 85
   Wm., 86
Polk
   Ezek., 83
   Thos., 83
   Will, 83
Pollock
   Cullen, 17
   Cullen, Esqr., 15
Pollocks
   Cullen, 150
Pollok
   Cullen, 26
Port Brunswick, 69
Port Roanoke, 81
Porter
   Jas, 83
   Robert, 83
Portuguese
   Mena Portagees, 8
Pound
   John, 130
Powel
   J, 97
   John, 97
   John Esqr., 97
Powell
   Mr., 78
   Mr. James, 78
   William, 148
   William Senr., 147
   Wm. Senr., 148
Pratt
   William, 4
   Wm., 5, 6
Price
   Isaac, 83
   John, 67
   Jonathan, 67
Pruhar[?]
   Benjamin, 66
Pugh
   Thomas Whitmell, 58
   Thomas Whitmill, 59
   Thos, 59
   Thos., 58
Purviance
   William, 122, 125, 139
   Wm., 123
Pyles
   P., 31

Q

Quakers, 54, 64, 65, 74, 75
   On the emancipation of slaves, 64
   Protest slavery, 54
Quince
   John, 127
   Parker, 38

Index

R

Raboun
  Matthew, 13
Rail
  Geo., 67
Ramsays
  Mr., 115
Ramsey
  Robert, 83
Randall
  William, 32
Ransom
  James, 123, 124
Rasor
  Edward, Sheriff, 10
Ratliff
  Cornelius, 66
  Richard, 66
Rea
  Jno., 83
Reaford
  Philip, 84
Reasonover
  Joseph, 145
Reddick
  Mills, 132
  Mr. Mills, 131
Reding
  Joseph, 129
  Trimagain, 129
Reece
  Caleb, 66
Reed
  James, 83
  William, 129
Reep
  Thos., 31
Relfe
  Thomas, 37
Respess
  Thos, 134
Respess[?]
  Thomas, 134
Reynolds
  David, 66
  Jeremiah, 66
Rhodes
  Henry, Sheriff, 16, 18
Rice
  Jno., 6
  Mr. John, 4
Rich
  John, 66
  John, Jr., 66
Riddick
  Mr. Mills, 132
Rieusset
  John, 100, 101, 102
  John Esqr., 101
Rieussets
  Mr., 100
Rivers
  Cape Fear, 28, 125
  New River, 99
  North East, 125
Roanoke
  Port of, 49
Roberts
  Holston, 141
  John, 8
  Shadrach, 28
  William, 118
  WIlliam, 118
  Willis, 28
Robeson
  James, 64
  Thos, 83
Robinson
  Wm., 67
Rodgers
  John, 83
  Matthew, 83
  Wm., 83
Rogers
  Jacob, 67
  Julin, 140
Rouse
  Alexr., 140
Routledge
  Tho., 111
  Thomas, 132
  Thos, 133
Rudduck
  John, 65
Rudduk
  John, 65
Ruffin
  Samuel, Sheriff, 16
Russ
  Hezekiah, 12, 13
Russel
  Wm., 38
Russell
  William, Esqr., 37
Russill
  Tim, 67
Rust
  John, 31
Rutherford
  General, 160
  Genl., 72
  Jno., 73
  john, 107
  John, 72, 73, 87, 107
  John, Esqr., 73
  John, his brother and sister sent to Europe, 73

Index

Mr, 27
Mr. Griffith, 27
Thomas, 72, 73
Willm. Gordon, 72
Rutledge
  Thos, 111
Rynchy
  Jane, 132

S

Saltar
  Olivr., 96
Salter
  Oliver, 95
  Thomas, 83
  Willm., 22
Saltworks, 45
Sampson
  James, Clerk of Court, 17
  Jas., 133
  John, 132, 133
Sanders
  [Faded], 66
  David, 66
  Hezekiah, 66
  Jesse, 31
  Joel, 66
  John, 66
Saunders
  Colo., 158
Savage
  Lovelace, 62
Sawyer
  John, 129
  Lemuel, Sheriff, 10
  Mr., 64
Schaw
  Robert, 89

Robt., 87, 88
Schooley
  Saml., 66
Schooners
  Betsy, 69
Scipper
  George, 97
Scott
  Andr., JP, 6
  Robt, 57
Scott[?]
  Doctor, 5
Scull
  Capt., 159
Searcy
  Reuben, CC, 56
Secretary of State Papers, 94
Sessums
  Isaac, 61
  Jacob, 61
  Solomon, 61
Shannen
  James:, 83
Shehan
  Thomas, 58, 59
  Thos, 59
  Thos., 58
Simmons
  A.B., 145
  Emanuel, 32
  Eml., 144
Simpson
  Charles, 101
  John, Sheriff, 13
  Mr., 100
Singeltary
  Richard, 103, 104
Sitgraves
  J., 40
  J., CS, 39, 40
  John, CS, 39

Sitgreaves
  Jno., Sp, 81
Siviret
  Robert, 143
Sivreat
  Robert, 144
Skinner
  Evan, 143
  Mr. Jonathan, 77
Slaves
  Absey, 53
  Aggy, 53
  Alexander, 88, 90, 91
  Alexander Day, emancipated slave, 91
  Amelia, 89, 91
  an outlawed Slave, 38
  Andrew, 50
  Annis, 134
  Arthur, 145, 146
  Bacchus, 19
  Baccus, 26
  Backus, 23
  Ben, 16
  Betty, 88, 89, 91
  Bill of emancipation, 91
  Boatswain, 38
  Boston, 18
  Caesar, 77
  Caesar, emancipated, 77
  Caesar, emancipation of, 76
  Cain, 103
  Casar, 131, 132

Index

Cato, 17, 23, 107, 113, 114, 147, 148
Cato, an outlawed slave., 9
Ceasar, 76
Cesar, 10, 149, 150
Charles, 4, 5, 6, 16
Cloe, 108
Cudgoe, who was outlawed, 22
Cudjo, 19, 125
Cuff, 130, 135
Cyrus, 7
Daniel, 123, 124
Davie, 2
Dick, 5, 12, 13, 18, 19, 116
Dublin, 11
Duties on slaves, 68
Elisha, 53
Emancipation Bills, 89
Emelia, 87
Essex, 2, 128, 129
Esther, 70, 71, 142, 143
Gallaway, 85
Galloway, 86
Georg, 3
George, 132, 133
Gibby, 138
Golaway, 85
Golaway, runaway, 85
Hannah, 46, 60
Harry, 23
Hercules, 149

Hiring out of, 34
Importation of from Africa, 80
Importation tax of, 80
Isaac, 138, 139
Ismael, *99*
Jack, 6, 8, 9, 20, 21, 46, 60, 84, 100, 101, 121, 122
Jacob, 59
James, 40
Jamy, 79
Jemmy, 10, 11, 21
Jim, 39, 61, 139, 140
Jim, a Molatto lad, 61
Joe, 12
John Brown, 20
Johnney, 22
Johnny, 120, 121
Josey, 98
Liberated, 88
Liberation of, 75
Limerick, 79
London, 15, 118
Lucie, 88
Lucy, 89, 91, 134
Luke, 14
Lymus, an outlawed slave., 63
Manumitted, 74
Mariah, 108
Mary, 110, 111
Morrise, 9
Moses, 15, 17
Ned, 123, 124
Nedd, 2

Negro Will, 1
Nero, 24, 25
Outlying Rebel Slaves committing feloneys and attempted murder, 51
Patience, 74, 75
Peter, 17, 63, 110, 128, 129
Phiba. *See* Phoebe
Phill, *97*
Phillis, 134
Phillis, who was a runaway and outlawed, 21
Phoebe, 110
Pompey, 13, 14, 114
Prince, 105, 144
Priss, 74, 75
Quamino, 21, 119
Quash, 118
Quaugh, 7
Rachel, 74, 75
Rebel slaves, 51
Richard, 88, 90, 91
Richard Day, emancipated slave, 91
Robin, 21
Rose, 13, 108, 140
Sam, 13, 62, 63, 74, 75, 151
Sam L., 108
Sambo, 10
Sampson, 7

Index

Samuel Johnson, emancipated slave, 91
Scipio, 95, 96
Seip, 135, 136
Selah, 74, 75
Serina, 105, 106
Simon, 15, 17, 63, 143, 149
Ste[Smudged], 108
Stephen, 100, 101, 102
Sue, 151
Swift, 55, 56
Tartola Prince, 43
Thomas, 89
Thomas Clinch, 90, 91
Titus, 140, 141
Titus, outlawed, 12
Toddy, 15, 17
Tom, 3, 6, 8, 9, 20, 58, 108, 109, 112
Tonay, 78
Toney, 56, 57, 127, 139, 146
Toney, a runaway, 56
Tony, 3
Will, 1, 22, *102*, 122, 127, 128, 138
Small
  Obediah, Junr., 66
Smith
  Guy, 31
  John, 28, 58, 59, 66, 131, 144

Josiah, 58, 59
Saml., JP, 58
Samuel, 31, 55
Stephen, 137
W., 83
Snelen
  Agula, 28
Snoad
  Henry, 105
  Snoad, 105
Sother
  John, 67
Spaight
  Mr., 64
  Richard, Esqr., 9
Spalding
  Henry, 31
Sparrel
  Wm., 101
Spaulding
  Charles, 28
  Henry, 28
Speed
  Joseph, 62
  Joseph, CC, 61
Spencer
  Edward, 37, 38
Spicer
  Mr. John, 34
Springer
  Stephen, 67
St. George
  Geo., 140
St. Vincent
  Negroes imported from, 36
Standing
  Hend:, 131
  Henderson, 131
Standley
  David, Sheriff, 26
Stanfield

Wm., 67
Stanley
  David, Sheriff, 23
  Micajah, 67
  Saml., 67
  Strangaman, 67
  Wm., 67
Stanton
  Benjamin, 66
  Samuel, 66
Starbuck
  Gayer, 67
Starkey
  Edward, Sp, 52
  Edward, Sp., 49, 51
Starky
  John, 99
Starns
  David, 83
  Frederick, 83
State Troops, 82
States
  Georgia, 68, 69
  South Carolina, 82, 87, 149
Steed
  Jesse, 158
Stephens
  Even, 67
Stevenson
  John, 83
Stewart
  Alexr., 135
  Jehu, 66
  John, 83
Stier
  Joseph, 83
Stokes
  Mr., 72
Stone
  Frdk., 58, 59

Index

Mr., 64
Zedekiah, 58, 59
Stovall
  Barthw., 31
  Drury, 31
  George, 31
  John, 31
  Josiah, 28
  Josie, 31
Stringer
  Frances, 97
  Frs., 97
Styerin
  William, 30
Sumner
  Colo., 153
  Jethro, 123, 124
  Moses, 115
Sumpter
  Brigadier Genl., 82
Swift
  Sam., 118
  Sam:, 114
  Samuel, 113, 118
Symond
  Abram, 129
Symons
  John, 67
  John, Junr., 67

T

Tabb
  Thomas, 147
Talbot
  Jno., 66
Tatem
  John, 112
Tatlock
  Edward, 66
Taylor
  Luke, 131
  Mr. Ralph, 110
Taylors
  Ralph, 111
Thims
  Christopher, 28
  William, 28
Lee, 101
Thomas
  Saml., Executers of, 20
Thomes
  Rd., 31
Thomson
  Margaret, 107
Thornbrough
  George, 66
  Henry, 65
  James, 67
  Jos., 67
  Tho., 67
  Tho., junr., 67
  Thos, 66
  Walter, 66
Thornton
  John, 123, 124
Thorntons
  John, 25
Thrift
  James, 146
Tisdale
  Mr, 33
  Mr., 32, 33
  William, 32, 33, 45
  William, Esqr., 32
  William, Notary Public, 88
Tites
  Denis, 83
Tomlinson
  Edge, 32
  John Edge, Memorial of, 32
  Josiah, 66
  M, 32
  Mr, 33
  Mr., 32
  Samuel, 65
  Wm., 65
Tony
  Richard, 66
Toomes
  Joshua, 108
Treasurer and Comptroller Papers, 94
Tripp
  William, 134
Trippe
  Willm., 134
Trueblood
  Caleb, 66
  Josiah, 67
Tryon
  William, 29
  Wm., 27
Tucker
  Robert, 112
  Robert Junr., 112
  Robt, 112
Tudor
  Jno, 28
Turnbull
  Thomas, 107
Turner
  Edward, 104
  Gilbert, 104
  James, 96
  Thomas, 123
  Thos., 124
  Wm., 104

Index

Turner, Mrs.
  William, 96

U

Underhill
  Joseph, 142, 143
Unthenk
  Allen, 67

V

VA County
  Norfolk, 111, 112
  Pittsylvania, 154
VA Towns
  Petersburg, 154
  Peytonsburg, 154
  Williamsburg, 113
Vaughan
  Thomas D., 22
Veall
  George, 112
  Thomas, 112

W

Wade
  Joseph, 31
  Richard, 30
Waggenor
  William, 105
  Wm, 105
Wahob
  Israll, 83
Wahole[?]
  James, 83
Walker
  Andw., 83
  James, 26
  Jno., 85
  John, 83, 84, 85, 119, 120, 121
  John, Sheriff, 11
  Major John, 86
  Mr. John, 7
  Mr. William, 7
  Thomas, 83
Wallis
  Wm., 28
Ward
  Anth., 123
  Anthony, 119, 120, 121, 122, 127
  Benjamin, 130
  Capt. Ben, 25
  Edwd., 99
  Enoch, former Sheriff, 12
  Mary, 130
  Richard, 18
  Robert, 148
  Timothy, 66
Warran
  Henchee, 141
Warren
  Henchee, 141
Warwick
  John, 135
Watters
  Mr. Joseph, 6
Weaver
  John, Sheriff, 19
Weight &
  Mortimore, 7
Welch
  John, 83
Weldon
  Samuel, 46, 59, 60
  Samuel, Esqr., 46
Wesley
  William, 83
West
  William, 59
West Indies, 35
Wheeler
  Jonathan, 65
White
  Benjamin, 66
  Caleb, 66
  Francis, 65
  Isaac, 28, 31
  James, 66
  Jesse, 67
  Jordan, 67
  Josiah, 67
  Thomas, 66, 67, 84
  Thos., 104
  Toms, 65
  Wm., 65
Whitehead
  Benja., 31
  Saml., 31
  William, 31
Whitlock
  George, 28
Whittington
  Thomas, 28
Whorton
  William, 28
Wickersham
  Jehu, 66
Wike
  Philip, 83
Wilcox
  John, 31, 34
Wilkerson
  John, 28
Wilkins
  Joseph, 142, 143

Index

Wilkinson
  William, 119, 120, 122, 123
  Wm., 121
Williams
  Edward, 10
  Henry, 40
  Isaac, 66
  J., 83
  James, 5
  Jesse, 67
  John, 30, 83, 101
  Matthias, 67
  Mr Henry, 138, 139
  Mr., 76
  Mr. Henry, 138
  Obed, 140, 141
  Richd., 67
  Silas, 67
  Steph., 141
  Stephen, 140
  William, 31
  Wm., 2, 65
Williamson
  James:, 28
  Martha, 124
  William, 123, 124
Williamsons
  William, 25
Willis
  Augustin, 59, 60
  Augustine, 46
  Joseph, 31
  William, 105
  Wm, 105
Willoughby
  Lemuel, 112
Wilson
  Isaac, 66
  Jacob, 67
  Jesse, 66
  Joseph, 66
  Reuben, 67
Winchester
  Daniel, 83
Windley
  Aaron, 134, 135
Winslow
  Jacob, 65
  John, 66
  Mr., 67
Wood
  Mr., 90
Woodard
  John, 134
Woodby
  Thomas, 95
Woods
  John, 134
Woodward
  Abraham, 66
Wooten
  William, 60
  William, CC, 60
  Wm., 146, 148
  Wm., CC, 60
Wootten
  Wm., CC, 46
Worley
  Lois, 149
  Lowes, 150
Worsley
  Mary, 135
Worth
  Daniel, 66
  Job, 66
  John, 66
  Joseph, Junr., 66
  Silas, 66
Wright
  Capt. Stephen, 112
  Captain Stephen, 112
  Moore, 63
  Ralph, 66
Wylee
  John, 83
Wynns
  Benjamin, 14, 115
  Benjn., 115
  Mr., 68, 90

Y

Yancey
  Charles, 55
  Chas., 31
  James, 31, 55
  Lewis, 55
  Lewis, Esqr., 55
  Philip, 31
  Thomas, 31
Yates
  Richard, 13
Yeargain
  Samuel, 76
Yeargan
  Samuel, 76, 77
  Samuel, Will of, 77
Yeates
  Richard, 114, 115
Yonge
  C., 68
  Christian, 68
Younce
  Robart, 83
Young
  Christian, 69
  John, 31, 55
  Thornton, 31

Other Heritage Books by William L. Byrd, III:

Against the Peace and Dignity of the State: North Carolina Laws Regarding Slaves, Free Persons of Color, and Indians

Bladen County, North Carolina Tax Lists: 1768 through 1774, Volume I

Bladen County, North Carolina Tax Lists: 1775 through 1789, Volume II

For So Long as the Sun and Moon Endure: Indian Records from the North Carolina General Assembly Sessions, & Other Sources

In Full Force and Virtue: North Carolina Emancipation Records, 1713–1860

North Carolina General Assembly Sessions Records: Slaves and Free Persons of Color, 1709–1789

North Carolina Slaves and Free Persons of Color: Chowan County, Volume One

North Carolina Slaves and Free Persons of Color: Chowan County, Volume Two

North Carolina Slaves and Free Persons of Color: Pasquotank County

North Carolina Slaves and Free Persons of Color: Perquimans County

Villainy Often Goes Unpunished: Indian Records from the North Carolina General Assembly Sessions, 1675–1789

Other Heritage Books by William L. Byrd, III and John H. Smith:

North Carolina Slaves and Free Persons of Color: Burke, Lincoln, and Rowan Counties

North Carolina Slaves and Free Persons of Color: Hyde and Beaufort Counties

North Carolina Slaves and Free Persons of Color: Iredell County

North Carolina Slaves and Free Persons of Color: Mecklenburg, Gaston, and Union Counties

North Carolina Slaves and Free Persons of Color: McDowell County

North Carolina Slaves and Free Persons of Color: Stokes and Yadkin Counties

ABOUT THE AUTHOR

WILLIAM L. BYRD, III has been involved in genealogical and historical research for more than thirty years. His primary areas of interest are Native Americans, African Americans, West Indians, East Indians and Moors in Virginia, North Carolina, and South Carolina.

He has been published by the *North Carolina Genealogical Society Journal*, the *Magazine of Virginia Genealogy*, *The Rowan County Register*, and *The South Carolina Magazine of Ancestral Research*. He has also co-authored articles with Sheila Stover in the *North Carolina Genealogical Society Journal*, *The Augustan Society Omnibus*, the *Pan-American Indian Association News*, and the *Eagle: New England's American Indian Journal*. He has received an "Award of Special Recognition" from The North Carolina Society of Historians in the category of "The History Article Award" for preserving North Carolina history.

He is a U.S. Army Veteran from the Vietnam era, and served with the U.S. Armed Forces overseas. He is currently retired, and resides with his family in Hickory, North Carolina.

www.ingramcontent.com/pod-product-compliance
Lightning Source LLC
Chambersburg PA
CBHW051047160426
43193CB00010B/1090